Contemporary Quilts

Design, Surface and Stitch

Contemporary Quilts

Design, Surface and Stitch

Sandra Meech

B T Batsford

Acknowledgements

I would like to thank friends and colleagues for their contributions to this book and Michael Wicks for his wonderful photography. This book is dedicated to my parents Eric and Truda Tritton, who have always encouraged and supported my talents, and to my art teacher, Finlay Mackenzie, for his inspiration and enthusiasm years ago. Most of all, I would like to thank my family, Darryl and Warren, who have kept my feet on the ground over the last year.

First published 2003
Reprinted 2004 (1st), 2004 (2nd), 2005

© text and images Sandra Meech 2003

The right of Sandra Meech to be identified as Author of this work has been asserted by her in accordance with the Copyright, Designs and Patents Act 1988.

Volume © B T Batsford 2003

Photography by Michael Wicks

ISBN 0 7134 8856 5

A CIP catalogue record for this book is available from the British Library.

Printed in Malaysia by Times

for the publishers
B T Batsford
The Chrysalis Building
Bramley Road
London W10 6SP

www.chrysalisbooks.co.uk

An imprint of Chrysalis Books Group plc

Distributed in the United States and Canada by Sterling Publishing Co., 387 Park Avenue South, New York, NY 10016, USA

Page 1: **Spirits Soar**; *Page 2:* **Ice Floe (detail)**; *Page 3:* **Starry, Starry Night (detail)**; *Right:* **Remembering Cabot**. *All quilts by the author.*

Contents

Introduction

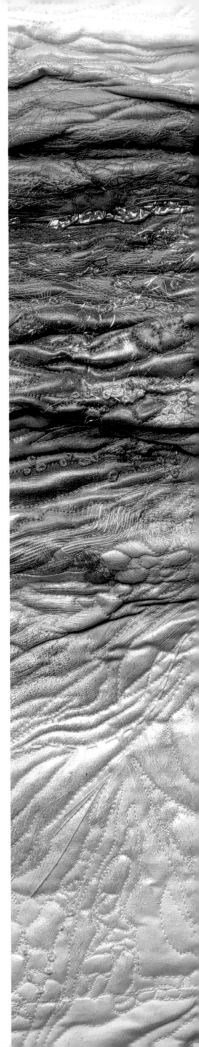

For centuries, layers of cloth have been stitched together to make quilted garments for protection and warmth. Later the same techniques were used to make bed coverings from used clothing and scraps of fabric. The American quilts that are so familiar to us originated from the 17th-century quilts that were taken by Europeans to North America. Here block piecing developed further, with countless patterns being created and new appliqué methods devised. Quilts remained in the bedroom until the mid-twentieth century, when the use of fibre and cloth took on a more expressive meaning. It was then that art quilts came into being.

Although fundamental piecing and quilting techniques remain the same, quilters now have the freedom to go beyond the geometric and symmetrical block pattern or ornate Baltimore appliqué styles and create something unique and personal. Quilt art, as this style is often called, now includes ways of creating fabric surfaces, painting, dyeing or transferring images to cloth, layering (using sheers or lace) and mixed media (including paper, plastics or metal) with the embellishment of mark-making threads, wools, metallics and beads. Contemporary quilts have left the bedroom and become wall art, a creative expression for today's quilters.

The biggest dilemma for most quilters is where to start when they want to break away from a traditional block or prescribed design and try something different and original for themselves. The goal of *Contemporary Quilts: Design, Surface and Stitch* is to build confidence in the quilter who already knows the basics of patchwork and quilting and who wishes to create their own designs. This book begins by identifying sources of inspiration and outlining ways to collect and develop sketchbook information on a given theme, and goes on to discuss the basic principles of design. You will be able to experiment with new ways of expressing yourself in paper and cloth, and then take this further with new ideas for stitch and embellishment. The Artist's Hints in every chapter give additional important information while the Design Classes provide valuable creative exercises along with unique worksheets that can be used time and time again.

Sit back and enjoy your quilt-making. Understanding the creative process and being given an opportunity to try something new for yourself will make anything possible.

Opposite page and right: **Arctic Landscape**
(Sandra Meech). Acrylic paintings photo-transferred and machine quilted through wireform, with scrim and copper added.

Using this book

This book is for quilters of all levels of skill – those who have no previous art or design experience but seek new ideas to extend their own creativity, or those who are continuing to meet new challenges and gaining confidence in the process. From the beginning, it is a journey, step by step, from sources of inspiration in the world around us, through design and colour theory, to ideas for surfaces, stitch and embellishment. It is a progression from source to stitch, with drawings and illustrations including a gallery of contemporary quilts.

Chapter by chapter

Chapter 1 is about finding an inspirational theme to work with, from choosing cameras and taking good photographs to learning how to isolate information with the use of viewfinders, coloured pencils and magazine papers.

Chapter 2 concentrates on creating painted surfaces on paper and cloth and using mixed-media collage with pattern and texture as the main focus. Collecting design information is important, so a Design Class about creating sketchbooks is included. Sketchbooks are always personal and individual and they can be a wonderful tool for self-expression as well as an invaluable place to start. This chapter also covers the method of transferring images onto cloth that I use in my quilts as well as transfer-dye techniques.

Chapter 3 reviews the basic rules and elements of design. A useful Artist's Hint shows how to create a design board by your desk, and the chapter's Design Class features a creative fabric and paper collage using rotated and repeated blocks as a starting point.

Chapter 4 is devoted to understanding the basic rules and theory of colour, fundamental to gaining confidence in design decisions for contemporary quilts.

Chapter 5 focuses on modern approaches to piecing and appliqué with a review of free machine embroidery, quilt mark-making and embellishment. A design-and-stitch project on inspired landscapes in this last chapter consolidates the surface and design approaches learned throughout this book.

You can determine your own pace as you move through the chapters. As you progress through the Design Classes you are encouraged to build your own working design file, gaining confidence in the process. Above all, you will discover that in contemporary quilting anything is possible, and that creative expression in contemporary quilt-making is available to everyone.

CHAPTER 1
INSPIRATION

Often we take the world around us for granted – the garden flower that bursts into bloom each spring or the buildings we pass every day. With trained eyes, these aspects of life and nature will take on new interest, as if we are seeing them for the first time. This first chapter looks at how life around us can motivate us to express ourselves uniquely, bringing something new and individual to our quilts and stitched textiles.

Inspiration

I have always been inspired by the world around me and I am constantly drawing, sketching or taking photographs of what I see. As a student at the Ontario College of Art in Toronto, I had an early opportunity to live in a bustling city, seeing the beauty of old buildings, the clean lines of modern architecture, the market stalls, Chinatown and the day-to-day life of its inhabitants. As a quilter, ideas come from every aspect of the everyday environment and the new and different places visited.

Over the years my own work has been highly influenced by travel – for example, the trip I made to the Inuit communities in Arctic Canada to study caribou-skin clothing and revel in the landscape in spring, seeing the tundra as the ice and snow melted to reveal the dormant earth beneath. I was able to meet the seamstresses and learn about their textiles and clothing. This has inspired many stitched textiles and quilts. *The Five Days in May: Pages from an Arctic Journal* (page 112), which depicts rock, ice, skin, hamlet and tundra in long panels, is about my experiences during the visit and Inuit stories expressed through photography and fabric. Recently, travel and photography have combined again in a new design series that I called *Journeys*, which takes a closer look at the way we live in both city and countryside in Canada, the USA and Europe. In *The Way We Live Now* (opposite page and right) the places we live in were the inspiration. Here are some sources that might spark off fresh ideas:

Holidays

Travel gives us an opportunity to enjoy different landscapes and architecture, see unfamiliar plants and animals, try a different cuisine or explore new cultures and textile traditions. We have time for relaxation, an opportunity to take photographs, write and sketch our observations and record thoughts and ideas for the future.

Home

Often our best sources of inspiration are on our own doorstep. Perhaps it is a plant in the garden that gives pleasure year after year or a particular view enjoyed in every season, showing nature at its best and worst. It could be the local church steeped in beauty and history, colourful fruit and vegetables on market day, the view from a high-rise office building, a blend of old and new architecture against a richly tinted sunset or just daily life as it passes by.

We are also strongly motivated by our ideals and emotions including family bonding, happy memories of childhood, celebrations of life, our parents, our children or even feelings of isolation, sadness and despair. Our loves, our hates, our vices and our humours are all part of what is important and unique to each of us and can all be sources of new ideas for our work.

Opposite page and right: **The Way We Live Now** *(Sandra Meech). Atlantic City, Spain, Monaco, Ontario, St. Johns (Newfoundland), Chicago. Holiday memories: homes briefly visited, never forgotten. All panels are linked with a central design element: photos, diary writing and painted or printed cloth.*

Where do we find inspiration?

The natural world

In nature we can find some of the best starting points for creativity. The natural world is often the first area looked to for interpretation when we want to move from a traditional block approach. With some basic piecing techniques or appliqué, any of the following themes would make wonderful contemporary quilts.

Landscapes give us huge vistas with distant views or detail in the foreground. These can be anything from lush tropical vegetation or atmospheric mountain scenes to hot, arid deserts.

Weather can bring us wonderful sunsets, big skies, clouds, mists and extremes in climate – rainbows, hurricanes, snow, sleet and rain.

The four seasons, another popular theme, reflect change, colour, new life, growth, fruit, ripening, harvest, decay and death.

Details in nature can be appreciated in gardens, either wild or formally designed, with a multitude of flowers, shrubs and trees. Look at texture in bark, pattern in leaves, moss and lichen or the colour, structure and shape of rock.

A closer look at nature reveals seedpods, cobwebs, snowflakes, ice crystals and fossils, to name a few.

Wildlife gives us tropical fish, insects, butterflies, birds and large mammals, all with a huge spectrum of colour, pattern and design possibilities. As these are living creatures, movement and change factor into the equation.

The human figure cannot be forgotten. Used as a resource through the centuries by fine artists, figure and form are a part of the inspiration behind many contemporary quilts.

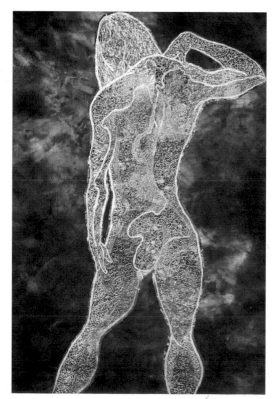

Right: **Life Class** *(Penny Berens, Canada).*
Dyed cotton with machine quilting and embroidery.

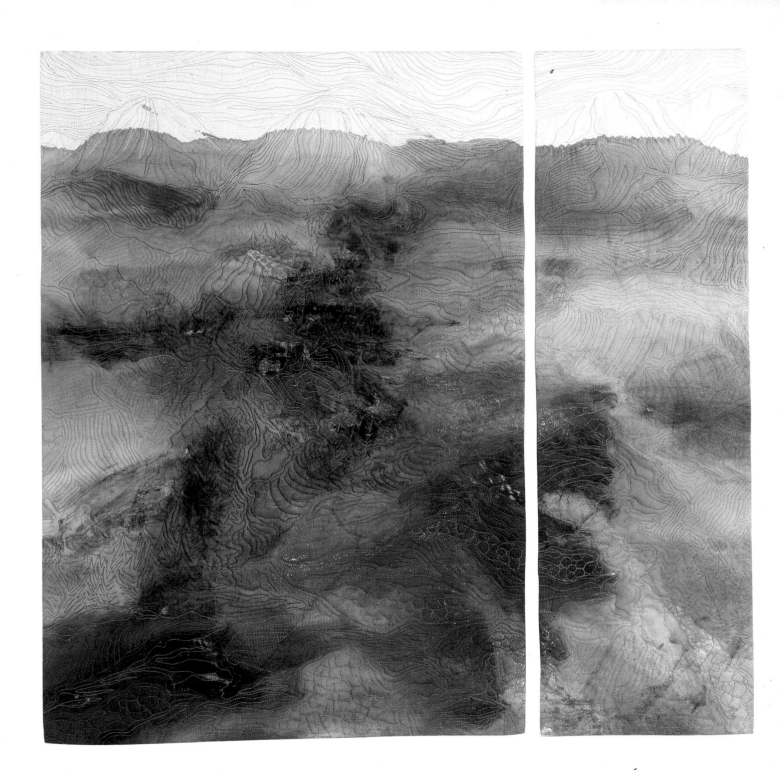

Above: **Winter Mist** *(Sandra Meech). Acrylic paint on cotton, machine quilted with iridescent paint added.*

Man's influence on the world

Through the ages man has produced art to reflect his effect on the world. This may include our dominance over nature, creating order in the landscape, or just telling the stories of our lives. This can be broken down into many different themes, all of which can inspire us.

Art and architecture are all around us – in buildings, both traditional and modern, at home and abroad. Modern buildings with reflecting glass stand proud on a skyline, or you might favour views of different villages around the world – African mud huts or adobe houses in the Middle East, both of which are full of interesting design and pattern potential. Think of details too, of stonework and sculpture, tiled floors and stained-glass windows. Consider ornament through the ages – Greek, Roman, Baroque, Renaissance, Victorian, Art Deco or whatever other style inspires you.

Historical symbols, heraldry and stories of myth and legend can also motivate new work. We should be careful not to reproduce art that has been created by others but use the essence of the original or a section of it – perhaps in an abstract form – in our own work.

Textiles and clothing continue to influence themes in contemporary quilts – consider the design and detail of the past as well as the modern fabric designs that we use today. Fabric coverings from remote regions of the world can be rich and colourful with heavy pattern and texture, influencing a design or style. In addition, costume, decoration and beadwork influence our choices for embellishment and stitch in our quilts.

Opposite page: **Room with a View** *(Sandra Meech). Marble floors and tiled roofs mix with sunflowers and the art and architecture of Tuscany. Photo transfer with fabric dyes.*
Above, left and right: Sketchbook memories of ceramic tiles and floor designs from Florence.

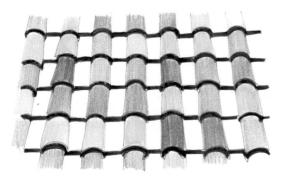

Above left and right: **Poster Mural 7** and **Roman Walls**
(Charlotte Yde, Denmark). From a series of wall collages.

Commerce and industry as a design source can bring to light a new way of looking at vehicles, hubcaps, manhole covers, wrought-iron fences, bicycles, shoes, clothing and jewellery. Perhaps machine parts, the workings of a clock or mechanical toys could inspire you.

Urban landscapes seen from a distance or from the air reveal road patterns and urban sprawl that can take on new beauty when seen in design terms. Ordnance Survey maps are a favourite design source of mine for machine quilting: the symbols and contour lines can inspire hand-stitched marks.

Ecological matters, although subjective, can motivate some strong work. We are all moved by current affairs and the effect man is having on the environment. War, famine, endangered species and climate changes have all been depicted in quilts in the past and will continue to be emotive subjects in the future.

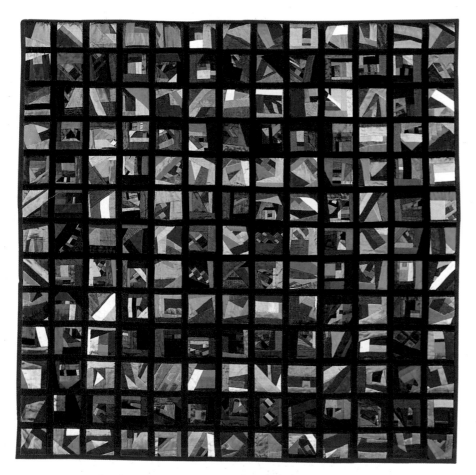

Opposite page: **Downland Study III** *(Carol Mowat, UK). Abstract lines and structures based on an ancient landscape. Acrylic on cloth, reverse appliqué with machine and hand stitch.*

Above: **Enmeshes VIII: Sunshine and Shadow** *(Sally-Ann Boyd, UK). Mixing old and new: modern squares with crazy patchwork centres.*

Emotions and feelings are also frequently seen as subject matter, particularly as women, who make up the majority of quilters, more freely express themselves on subjects close to family and home – birth, marriage, death, loss, joy, sadness, depression or health issues including breast cancer, AIDS or even a mid-life crisis. These ideas can be supported by descriptive words that document feelings, and intensified further by the choice of images and fabrics.

Colour and pattern on their own are strong influences in contemporary quilting and can be the sole inspiration for a new quilt. Working through the principles of colour can give wide-ranging results, creating different moods: calm or violent, soothing or aggressive.

Collage and creative surfaces can also provide a wonderful starting point for new work. In the next chapter we will be creating some wonderful painted papers that could be the basis for new ideas in design and pattern.

Above: **Broken Birds**
(Delia Salter, UK).
The title for this quilt came from a journalist's description of children damaged by war and three sisters (represented by the coloured silk in the three squares) living through sadness and pain.

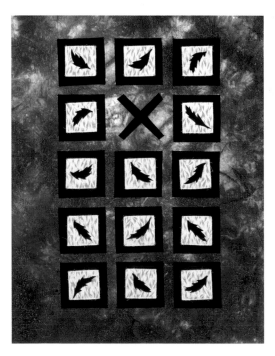

Left: **Broken Birds II** *(Delia Salter, UK).*
Childhood abuse is hidden within the safety of home with the symbolic 'kiss' or 'cross'.

Above: **Transition I** *(Jette Clover, USA).*

Urban walls represent layered and fragmented communication.

Collage of torn posters and scribbled messages.

COLLECTING INFORMATION

Often we keep coming back to a subject that intrigues us or a theme that is always in our thoughts and won't go away. It is important to pay attention and acknowledge this. This consuming interest could eventually become a series of quilts. Many contemporary quilting competitions already have themes that must be followed in order to qualify. Although they can be restrictive, these prescribed topics are open to interpretation and can often initiate an idea that would otherwise never be explored.

Sketchbooks and journals are a perfect way to collect information and ideas for future reference. Indeed, the best sources for our work are sketches and observations made on location. Whether it is a line drawing sketched at a museum, a landscape watercolour made on holiday or a still-life sketch produced in the garden, these small, workable records are invaluable, and they are even more potent when combined with words, which can often create better memories than a line drawing ever could.

There are a great number of ways to record impressions in a sketchbook: simple drawings, sketches, painted papers or collage (see Creating a Sketchbook, page 64). Working this way can sometimes be hampered by weather conditions, poor lighting or a lack of drawing materials or time. It is then necessary to record what we see with photography.

Opposite page: Sketches and photos depicting wonderful memories of Tuscany.
Below: Drawings taken from Charles Rennie Mackintosh designs.

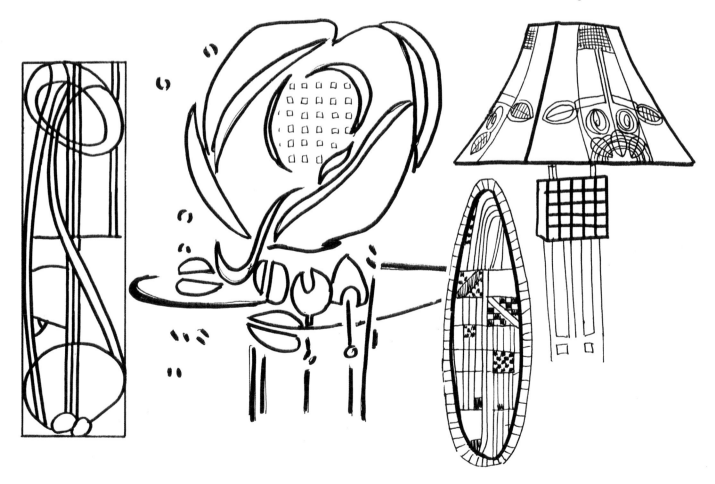

Above: Woven textures from Bolivia – a potential colour and design source.

Photography is an excellent way to collect information. Today, there are as many ways to capture good images as there are cameras to choose from, in a wide price range. The act of taking photographs helps you practise the techniques you will need to design a quilt. By isolating information in a frame and eliminating what you don't need, you can think about composition and colour at the same time. However, final photographic prints may not have accurate colour, so it helps to have coloured pencils handy to jot down true colour examples as well. Many quilters are also using their own photographs, transferred onto cotton, in their quilts.

Above: **Portrait of Dimitri** *(Diana Brockway, UK). This quilt was inspired by a woodcut from a Welsh folk legend.*

Books and magazines are the next best reference source. Copyright should never be a problem if you are only using this material as reference for your own design and not reproducing the image directly. There is always a great selection of magazines to choose from. *National Geographic* magazine is a favourite for landscape, nature photography and world cultures: people, art, textiles and architecture as well as scientific discoveries, ecological issues and urban living. Gardening, home-decorating and fashion magazines also include quality photographs, as do travel journals, books and holiday brochures that give an insight into places we might dream of visiting one day. Holiday postcards can also add to your file of information. Consider also a library visit that will allow access to illustrated reference books on every subject imaginable. Finally, don't forget the Internet as an invaluable resource.

Newspapers provide limited-quality photography and often only in black and white, but newspaper articles can give an edge to a modern theme, particularly one with emotive headlines and editorial comment. Many contemporary quilts include a collage of transferred images of news articles to give a punchy emphasis to a controversial subject. Also, old newspapers and advertising from the past with faded photographs and articles from a bygone era can work well.

Collectibles are available to many of us. Old photographs, letters and memorabilia, costume jewellery, stamps, colourful bottles, shells, pebbles and, of course, fabrics are all included in this category. Any of these could become the subject for that next quilt design.

Taking good photographs

Cameras come in many different guises so there is no reason why a reasonably good reference photograph isn't possible for anyone. Camera lenses on even the most basic models have improved and good detail and colour can be achieved in a 12.5 × 18cm (5 × 7in) print. Quality prints or transparencies of finished work for publication, exhibitions or juried selections are another matter, and a professional photographer may be needed.

Compact cameras are affordable, lightweight and small, and they often have a zoom facility for closer images and a built-in flash. Using standard 35mm film and with automatic settings it is a simple matter of point and shoot, and very good results can be achieved.

APS (Advanced Photo System) cameras are also lightweight and small. They give new film formats and print size possibilities, but film and processing can be expensive.

SLR (Single Lens Reflex) cameras give greater flexibility. The speed, aperture and focusing can be done manually or automatically. The variety of lenses gives greater choice – macro lenses for detail, wide-angle lenses for landscape, and zoom lenses for flexible image sizes. Adding filters will provide greater realism or artistic effects. A lightweight SLR with a 28–200mm lens (wide angle to zoom) is a good choice.

Digital cameras are the biggest camera innovation in recent years. The images are stored in the camera's memory and can be viewed and selected, then downloaded onto a computer. With photo-imaging software they can be enhanced, colour corrected and printed out on standard home printers with good results. High-resolution cameras, printing inks and photographic paper can be expensive but results are immediate and getting better all the time. This technology is here to stay and digital imaging is certainly the way forward.

Your camera choice is truly a matter of preference. If quality prints and slides are needed then a lightweight SLR looks like the best choice at the moment, otherwise a digital or compact camera would be a good alternative. You owe it to yourself to explore the full potential of your camera so consider getting hold of some photography books or joining an adult education course.

Artist's Hint | Photographic composition

Looking through the viewfinder of a camera isolates what you see, so taking photos is good practice for planning a quilt. The same rules of design apply.

1. For a landscape break the view into thirds and position your horizon line either two-thirds of the way to the top with interest in the foreground or on the lower third for drama.

2. Texture or pattern can dominate without a focal point, giving cohesive form to the photo.

3. Depth can be achieved with larger details in the foreground. Lines of perspective will take the eye deeper into the photo to mid-ground and background detail.

4. Colour can be used dramatically in large amounts as bold shapes or just a subtle hint for effect.

5. Framing a picture using design elements can help lead the viewer into and around the composition.

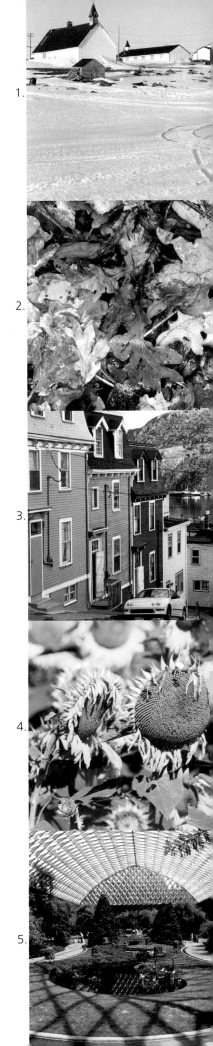

1.

2.

3.

4.

5.

Design Class 1 **Looking through a window**

Using a window aperture enables us to isolate or focus on an area of interest. This is one of the most valuable design exercises I know. Artists use their thumbs and forefingers to form a frame to look through when they sketch or paint. By eliminating other information we can really 'see' our subject, and focus on the colours within it more intensely.

For this first Design Class we will isolate an area in a photograph, determine the proportions of colour and follow a series of exercises using coloured pencils and cut magazine papers to translate this information. Choose a colourful photograph to begin with. A worksheet for this class can be found on page 125. Try these exercises several times – they will get easier each time and become invaluable starting points for future projects. This class and the others in this book will become an important file of design information to use as a resource in the creative process.

Materials

- A photographic reference that has 8–10 colours, including lighter or darker versions of one colour and neutrals like black, brown, or beige, if desired.

- Coloured pencils (a set of 24 is ideal).

- A copy of the design class worksheet on page 125.

- Magazines to cut up. (Interiors, gardening or style magazines work well).

- Thin card, 12.5 × 18 cm (5 in × 7 in).

- Paper scissors.

- Craft knife with cutting board.

- Glue stick.

Method

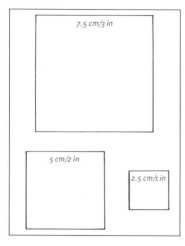

7.5 cm/3 in

5 cm/2 in

2.5 cm/1 in

1 Using a craft knife or paper scissors, cut templates from the card with 2.5cm, 5cm, and 7.5cm (1in, 2in, and 3in) square apertures.

chosen area

2 Choose a window depending on the size of the original and select an area. Think about colour for interest.

3 Carefully select 8–10 different coloured pencils to match the colours in the photograph. Think about the proportions of colour.

By really analyzing a section of your reference and being able to 'see' more colours you will also start looking at shape and texture as well. Think about using a collage of mixed media as a source of reference instead, or perhaps matching up your colour selection with rectangles of fabric.

4 The bar graphs provided on the worksheet have stripes in various widths. Fill them in using coloured pencils to match the amount of colour in your photograph (left), starting with the smallest amount of colour (perhaps the brightest) and working through to the largest portion. Include neutral colours such as black, brown, and beige if applicable.

5 Using the same selection of coloured pencils, fill in the grid of squares in a random way (right), in similar colour proportions to the bar graph you produced in step 4, starting with squares of the smallest colour and working to the largest.

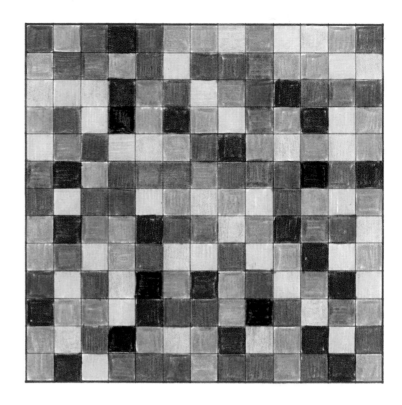

6 Lay the photograph to one side and find magazine papers in similar colours and proportions. Use pattern and texture for interest – these could resemble contemporary fabrics. Cut and paste sections onto the bar graph, leaving no white spaces between them (left).

7 With a similar combination of magazine papers, try weaving some in different widths for added inspiration (right).

The 'window' design exercise on these two pages, which was based on a photograph of the Arctic tundra in spring, resulted in **Spring Thaw** (Sandra Meech) (below right and detail on opposite page), a colourwash-style quilt created using photographic images and dyed, printed and commercial cotton. Breaking down colour proportions into a colour bar and random squares becomes a valuable first step in collecting the fabrics for any future project.

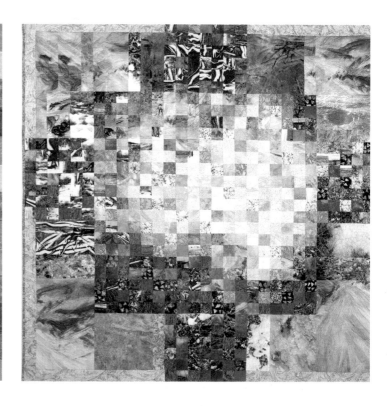

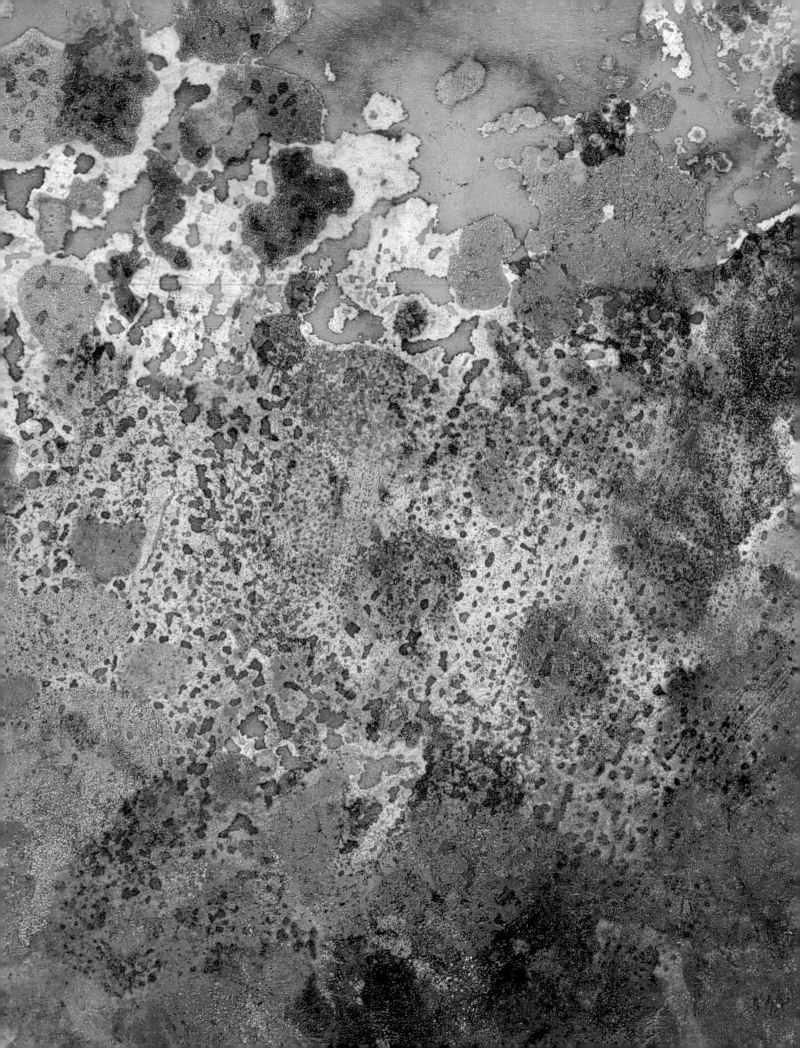

CHAPTER 2
SURFACES

Now that you have a subject or theme it is time to take the next step. It can be challenging and fun to create inspired surfaces on paper with drawing, painting and collage, or on cloth with dye and transfer effects, or using bonding and trapping techniques with plastics. This chapter will focus on the basic materials for making marks and creating these interesting coloured surfaces; backgrounds that could become the starting point for the next quilt project.

Opposite page: Melted wax crayon on cartridge paper (ironed between layers of parchment) and painted with dyes and inks.

Surfaces

Surfaces inspire us in so many different ways. Wonderful paint effects on paper can be taken further into cloth or photographic images can be transferred directly onto fabric. Quilters are no longer restricted to 100% cotton: paper, plastics and mixed media have all been included in contemporary quilts in recent years. Starting with sketchbook ideas, it is possible to progress through paint on paper and collage to dyed fabric and surface embellishment with plastic.

PAPER

There are many ways to decorate paper with pencils, crayons, pastels, paints, dyes and inks as well as collage techniques. You will find that experimenting with paper is a wonderful way to gain confidence with colour and design before moving on to fabric. Here are some ideas to get you started.

Drawing and mark-making

Drawing on paper or in sketchbooks needn't be an intimidating experience. Remember that sketching and recording information and ideas is a personal exercise and not designed to be viewed by others. It is a time to express and liberate yourself on paper before colouring fabric. Basic materials need not be expensive. Look at what you have already – you may be surprised.

It is important to record these surface techniques. They could be included in a notebook or sketchbook or form part of a working design file as an important reminder of the creative approaches that may be expanded into cloth in the future.

You may already have a subject from life or a photograph for inspiration. Working in pencil or fine pen to start with, fill the page with sketched detail and words of description. You will slowly want to move into colour and mixed media. If you find the bleak white of the paper intimidating, as many people do, then start with a wash of colour on the background, or use coloured papers. Think about light and shade for dimension, line for movement and sketchmarks for texture. Begin drawing on cartridge or sketching papers – any with a smooth surface. Alternatively you may wish to use watercolour paper for wash effects and Ingres paper for chalk pastels.

Opposite page: Paint and Pattern on white cartridge paper, including dyed paper with acrylic metallic paint stamped in a repeat pattern, contour lines with oil pastels and dye paint wash, and painted resists with wax crayon, candle wax and oil pastel. These patterns could be used as inspiration for piecing, appliqué and mark-making stitches.
Right: Beginning with a sketch – Michelangelo's David in Florence, using brown Conté pencil.

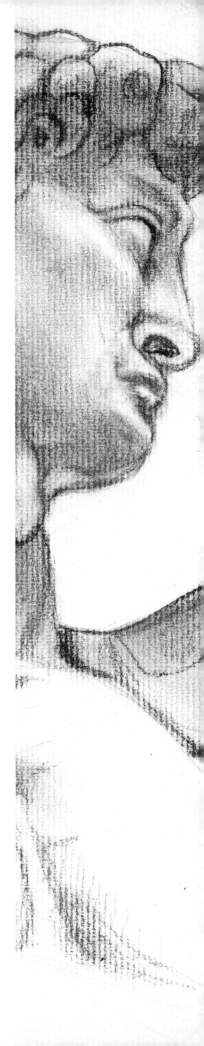

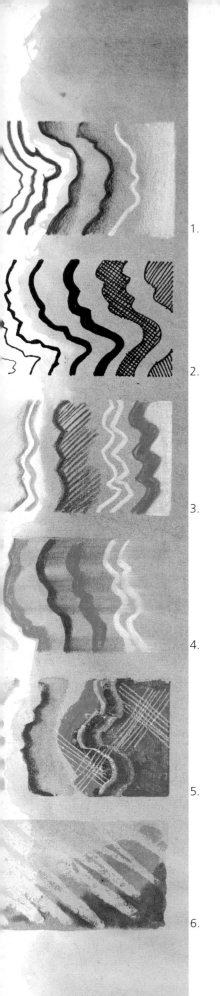

Try using the following materials:

Pencils You will need an HB, 2B and softer pencils (4B–8B) if desired, plus charcoal pencils in black and white for blending, a putty eraser for smudging and a craft knife or pencil sharpener.
▶ *Work several thicknesses of pencil line and add shading using white as a highlight (1).*

Pens Black fibre-tipped pens giving fine, medium and thick lines are useful for any subject.
▶ *Try making textures – parallel, wavy or crosshatch lines, circles or dots for pattern (2).*

Coloured pencils Soft, blendable pencils, preferably in a set of 24 or more for a good range of colour, are ideal for mark-making, creating textures or shading.
▶ *Experiment with your marks, and try using water-soluble or Aquarelle coloured pencils or sticks, which can be brushed with water to produce a wash (3).*

Chalk pastels and Conté pencils These give soft, muted effects when smudged with fingers or a cotton bud. Sketches will need to be sprayed with fixative for permanence. See if these suit your style of working (4).

Oil pastels These bright oil sticks give strong colours and are ideal for filling in large areas easily.
▶ *Try using them as a resist, painting over them with washes or to fill an area, blending or overlapping colour, then scratch or scrape into it for additional marks (5).*

Wax crayons Use these on their own or to create a resist under paint washes.
▶ *Try some pattern or repeat symbols, wavy or parallel lines of resist before painting (6).*

Right: Coloured pencils and a fine pen can produce interesting results.
Opposite page: Papers for dyeing and printing, including newsprint and handmade paper.

Acrylics

Acrylic paints come in many variations, in tubes or jars, and either thick or thin. All can be mixed with water. They are versatile, not too expensive and suitable for most surfaces. They dry quickly, are permanent, and are particularly good for use on paper and cloth. Many different colours are available, including iridescent, pearlized and metallic versions. Mixed with water, acrylics resemble watercolour or gouache, and they can also be painted on thickly with broad brushstrokes for a painterly effect.

Experiment with the paints, seeing what effects you can get by adding varying amounts of water. Try the following:

▸ *Create three-dimensional effects by adding artists' texture mediums, fine sand or beads.*
▸ *Mix in metallic powders for a dramatic effect and seal with a gloss or matt varnish.*

▸ *Spread thick acrylics on a glass plate, lay some paper face down on top and then press evenly with a roller to produce a monoprint. (Clean the glass immediately after use as the acrylic may be difficult to remove once dry.)*

Opposite page: Acrylic paint.
Above: Linocut of a Canada goose, printed onto cloth.
Below: Monoprint with fabric paints, used as background for **Woman with Ulu** *(Sandra Meech): dyed scrim, copper, photo image and stranded cotton stitch marks.*

Collage

Using painted papers is a pleasure. Forget children's craft papers for collage; we now have an endless array of painted papers and handmade papers to use. A good place to start is with symmetrical designs based on traditional blocks. Repeat patterns, mirror images or abstracted torn shapes will lead to interesting designs that could be developed further into an expressive wall hanging. Tearing paper gives an almost organic, natural look.

Try the following:

▸ *Arrange torn or cut geometric shapes such as circles, squares or triangles in a repeat formation.*
▸ *Weave strips of different widths through each other.*
▸ *Cut precise parallel strips, then cut and paste in a Seminole manner.*
▸ *Try a collage composition on a theme, using torn and cut magazine pictures. These are always more emphatic when words are included.*
▸ *Combine torn paper with thick acrylic paint and include photos and found objects for a mixed media example.*

▸ *Try pleating and folding papers to create three-dimensional effects. This is often seen in contemporary quilts.*
▸ *Experiment with tissue paper and glue: manipulate it, leave to dry and then paint it.*

Opposite page: Collage of torn, painted papers creating an evening Arctic landscape. Below left: repeated design with torn and cut paper. Below right: urban collage of photos and writings.

A variety of mixed media materials – paper, plastics and wire, for example – are often seen in contemporary quilts and textiles. When planning your own quilts, don't be afraid to experiment. A mix of painted and printed papers (magazines, newspapers and so on) can also be used directly as part of a quilt, but be aware of copyright laws: don't reproduce too much of the original work.

Painted papers can also be stitched when photocopied and transferred onto cloth (see page 57). Look at the colour, pattern and quality of the marks you have made that could translate into quilting stitches. The window template for Design Class 1 (page 24) will help you focus on an interesting area of your collage, which could be the starting point for a quilt.

Opposite page: **Tuscan Villa**
Collage with waxed and painted paper, gold tissue, and sketch details.
Above left: 3-D monochromatic papers and plastics woven and scrunched.
Above: A section of this paper collage could be the design source for a new project.

Opposite page: Brusho and ink dyes and acrylic on cartridge, textured and handmade papers plus newsprint. Metallic paint has been rubbed onto textured surfaces.

Above: **Bluebird** (Bente Vold Klausen, Norway). A quilt inspired by a photo of a dead bird and songs from childhood. Photo transfer with a collage of printed and painted textiles.

Left: Strips of painted and textured papers cut in a Seminole manner with added copper.

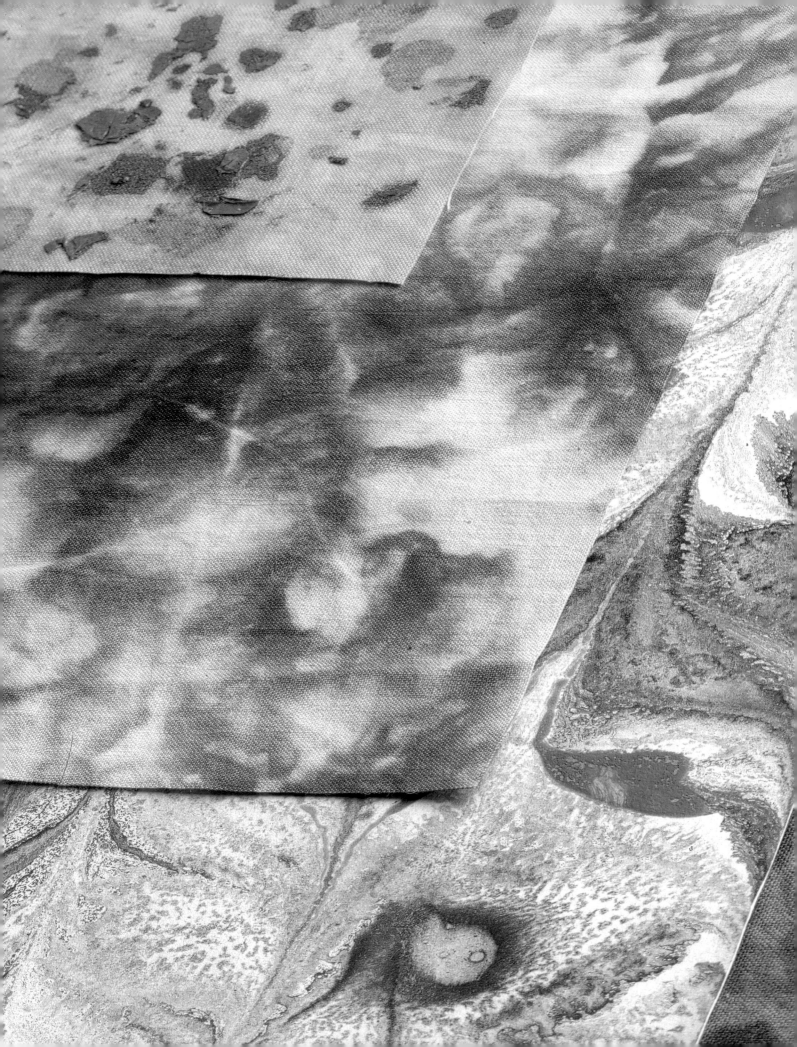

CLOTH

Traditionally quilters used recycled fabrics for their quilts. Today, every imaginable type of fabric is acceptable and a wonderful selection of plain colours and printed patterns are available to tempt us. These are most suitable for bed quilts, when regular washing is required, but today's quilters can use recycled fabrics as a base for creating their own dyed, painted or coloured surfaces for their contemporary quilts and wall hangings.

There are numerous ways of using paint and fabric dyes with cloth and as many books on the subject. Included here are three familiar approaches to colouring cloth – dyes, fabric paints and heat-transfer dyes – plus a description of photographic transfer techniques, which have also become popular. Adding plastics to these surfaces with the bonding and trapping of fabrics, paper and wool has also been included. Experimenting with new methods of creating fabric can be challenging and fun, and an opportunity to stretch boundaries.

Opposite page: Dyed and prepared fabrics.
Below: **...hanging on the wall** *(C. June Barnes, UK). A variety of natural fibres were machine appliquéd from the back, with free machine quilting, then the quilt was hand-dyed.*

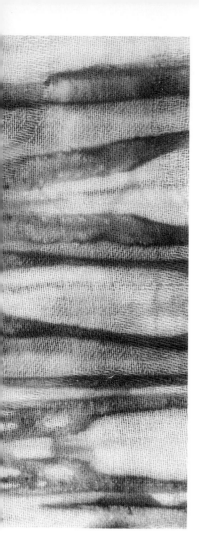

Dyes

Dyeing cloth is the oldest and most cost-effective way of colouring large amounts of fabric. A popular approach is using cold-water Procion dyes. These come in powder form in a basic range of hues that can be mixed to create every colour imaginable. They work best with 100% natural fabrics (like cotton, linen and silk), which must be washed first to remove sizing. Note that hand-dyed (and commercial) fabrics are light-sensitive and can fade in direct sunlight over time.

Method

Following the manufacturer's instructions, mix the dye powder and water to form a dye bath for the fabric and add a salt solution, which drives the dye into the fabric, and a soda solution, which fixes the dye. (Some manufacturers include salt and soda in their dyes.) After a period of time the colour is fixed and must be washed thoroughly in hot, soapy water until the water runs clear. Dyeing large amounts of fabric can take time and needs space, but there are other methods that are quicker, using plastic bags or a microwave (one which must be used only for dyeing fabric and not food preparation). Amazing results can be achieved with some of the more interesting dyeing methods. Here are some suggestions:

‣ *Try space-dyeing for crinkle or marble effects.*
‣ *Sprinkle rock salt on newly dyed fabric while it is still wet for texture and dimension.*
‣ *Experiment with tie-dying, batik or Shibori methods to give colour contrast and pattern.*

Above: African tie-dyed and batik cloth in wonderful colours and patterns can be effective.
Right: Sprinkling rock salt will draw out the dye colour to create an interesting pattern.
Far right: Space-dyeing creates marbled, scrunch-effect textures.
Opposite page: **Tresco** *(Ann Israel, UK). Exotic plants and palm trees on the island of Tresco were reproduced using indigo-dyed cottons pieced and applied to a recycled kimono lining.*

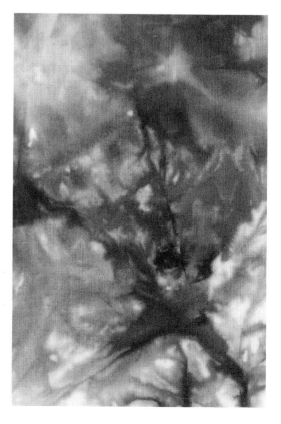

46

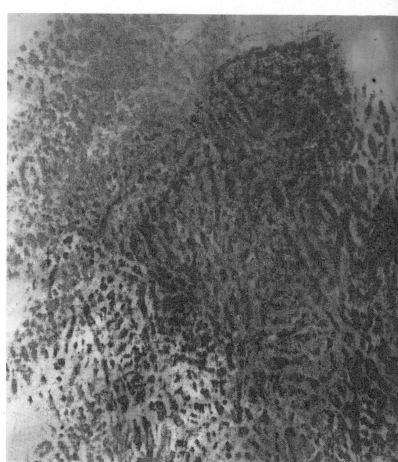

Fabric paints and sticks

Paints created especially for fabric are usually designed for either cotton or silk. Most are water-based and can be mixed together, and many are permanently set by using the heat of an iron or are steam-fixed. Some fabric paints will slightly stiffen fabric, but still allow for easy stitching.

Cotton fabric paints are applied in the same way as acrylic or dye paints on paper. Follow the manufacturer's instructions to fix it before washing. You may also like to try the following:

▶ *Overpaint white-on-white-patterned cottons for interesting results. Black and white fabrics also work well. The paint must be heat-set.*
▶ *Make your own sunprints by painting cotton, then placing shapes or forms such as leaves on top. Leave the cotton in direct sunlight for at least an hour for a print to appear.*

Silk paints are versatile, come in a large range of colours and are applied with a brush or sponge applicator. The paint spreads quickly across the fabric (silk or cotton), so a gutta resist is helpful for creating dividing lines between colours. It can be applied with a pipette, specially shaped bottle or brush and comes in a clear form or a basic range of colours. These resists can also thicken the consistency of the paint for stencilling, stamping or making other paint marks.

Paint sticks, for example Markal, are thick oil and wax sticks that enable painterly marks to be made on the surface. They can be applied freely or by using masking techniques. They come in a wide range of colours including metallic, iridescent and pearlized versions, take 48 hours to dry thoroughly and become permanent when heat-fixed. Stencilling paint sticks designed for home decorating are also worth a try.

▶ *Try masking areas for pattern or shape, then apply the Markal paint stick, dry thoroughly and iron to set.*
▶ *Place cotton over a textured surface and rub with a paint stick for interesting brass-rubbing style images.*

Top: Sunprint of a fern on white cotton using silk paints.
Above: Silk paints painted and heat-set on 'white on white' printed cotton.
Below: Paint sticks come in a full range of colours and are easy to use.

Opposite page far left: Silk paints in a tray for easy application.
Above right: Dyed cotton with Markal paint stick rubbed over a textured surface.
Below right: Acrylic on cotton with masked areas where Markal paint stick is applied.

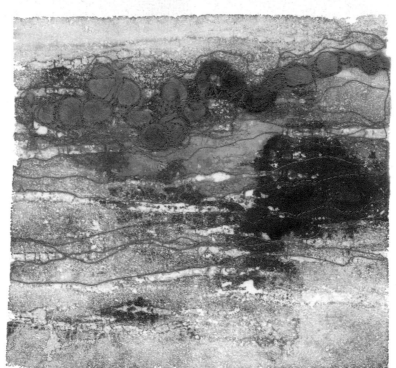

Left: Watered-down acrylic paint on a fusible web gives texture and dimension. Ironed onto cotton and machine stitched for embellishment, with no washing and ironing possible, these techniques are usually used in art quilt wall hangings only.

Acrylic paints are water-based and come in bottles or tubes. They have always been popular with quilt artists for adding interest to cloth surfaces and they can be painted on with broad brushstrokes or diluted for wash effects. Paint is absorbed into the cloth and will spread, but the use of an acrylic medium or extender will contain the colour to a particular area. Acrylic paint dries quickly and is permanent, but it can stiffen fabric considerably if paint is thickly applied and can affect the ease of quilting. You might like to experiment with the following techniques:

▸ *Make 'painterly' strokes on cotton, applying the paint diluted in some areas and thick in others.*
▸ *Try a monoprint. Use a roller to spread liquid acrylic paint evenly on glass and then make marks into it with a scraping tool (the hard end of a brush will do). Iron a piece of cotton onto freezer paper, then lay it fabric side down on the paint. Press over the whole paper with a clean roller and then pull off the print.*

▸ *Bondaweb (Wonder Under) is an iron-on fusible adhesive web used in appliqué. When the rough or glue side is painted with watered-down liquid acrylic, the backing paper shrinks as it dries to create interesting, organic patterns. When thoroughly dry, iron the painted side (including the backing paper) face down onto cotton, then after a few seconds gently peel off the paper. The surface may be tacky for a while but it will dry eventually. Never iron the finished material.*

Metallics and other specialist paints

add additional sparkle to dyed fabrics. There is a vast selection on the market including metallic, pearlized and iridescent paints. Some of these are textured to add an extra dimension and all will add lustre and sheen.

*Opposite page: **Containment** (Sandra Meech) is a comment on crowded urban living and confined spaces. Acrylic painted background with photo-transferred images, including sections with metallic fabrics and threads trapped in plastic.*

Transfer dyes

Transfer dyeing is another way of adding colour to surfaces for stitching. Transfer paints and crayons are easy to use. First draw or paint onto thin paper, then use the heat of a hot iron to transfer the image onto fabrics that have a high polyester content. It is possible to create a great variety of surface effects with this method, from crisp shapes to textural images. The colour range is adequate, but dyes can be mixed and blended to provide a wider choice. Supplied in premixed bottles or in powder form as disperse dyes, transfer dyes are water soluble and simple to use. I find that thin paper with a hard surface, such as artists' layout paper, is best for painting and heat transfer.

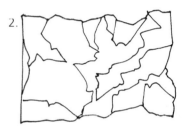

1.

To add variety to your work, try preparing the paper ready for transfer using one of the following methods:

▸ *Use resists such as candlewax, crayon or masking fluid to make lines and patterns before adding the transfer paint (1).*
▸ *Scrunch the paper before painting it. Paint diagonally across the page, giving movement to the final design (2).*
▸ *Tear and weave your transfer-painted papers, laying them face down onto the fabric before transferring them with a hot iron (3).*
▸ *Cut geometric shapes – circles, spirals, squares or triangles – in different colours and let them fall randomly onto the surface (4). Iron them in place where they fall. Place a background of a contrasting colour face down and iron with a high heat setting.*

Or you could try the following ideas:

▸ *Combine transfer paints and crayons. The crayons will add a new quality to the surface.*
▸ *Make silhouette images using leaves, threads, lace and so on for negative shapes.*
▸ *Apply the paint to Bondaweb (Wonder Under) for some interesting results. The paper backing shrinks when wet, so when you apply transfer paint to the glue side, wonderful patterns emerge as it shrinks. The whole piece can be ironed onto fabric, or the painted adhesive layer separated from the paper backing and used. Note that when ironing the glue side of Bondaweb you will need to protect the iron. Baking parchment or a Teflon sheet will both do the job. Keep the hot steam iron (used dry) moving as you transfer the image, otherwise steam holes will appear. Note also that if the exposed glue side of Bondaweb is pieced into a quilt it can't be ironed, so this surface is only appropriate for wall hangings.*

3.

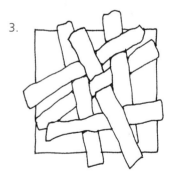

4.

2.

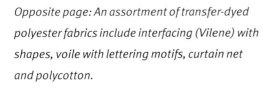

Opposite page: An assortment of transfer-dyed polyester fabrics include interfacing (Vilene) with shapes, voile with lettering motifs, curtain net and polycotton.

One of the most interesting aspects of transfer dyeing is that you can produce up to three prints from each example and you will find that the used dyed paper is interesting in its own right. Transfer-dyed fabrics are not completely colourfast and could fade in time, but their use as a background for collage materials and stitch is limitless.

Opposite page: **Starry, Starry Night** *(Sandra Meech). Stitched textile work with transfer-dyed polycotton background including cut star shapes, with layers of net and sheers plus stitched and trapunto quilting.*

Above: Transfer-dyed paper with first, second and third prints on polyester fabrics.
Right: Section of a collage including writing on transfer-dyed heavy interfacing. Wool and bonded plastics were added, then the fabric was machine stitched.

Photographs

There are several ways to transfer photographic images onto cloth to create your own fabric designs. Three of the popular techniques include using heat-transfer paper, a chemical called Bubble Jet Set 2000 and an acrylic medium such as Picture This or Image Maker.

Heat-transfer paper is designed to be used with a computer's printer and is marketed mainly for transferring images onto T-shirts. You can use a digital photograph, scanned image, typed words or computer-generated illustrations, but whatever you use it should be reversed or in a mirror image, because when it is transferred to the fabric it is reversed back again. The printed image should be transferred to white or cream cotton with a very hot, dry iron following the manufacturer's instructions. It is essential to move the iron constantly over the surface or steam holes will appear, and make sure you iron the edges as well as the middle for an even transfer. Images are adequate, although the cotton is stiffened. It may fade after several washings and it is not advisable to re-iron the image when piecing into a quilt. Nevertheless, this method has been popular for years.

Bubble Jet Set 2000 is a clear chemical that is infused into cotton fabric to create a surface that can be printed through a computer printer in the same way as paper. The fabric is soaked in the liquid in a flat tray and hung up to dry, then ironed onto freezer paper and trimmed accurately to fit into the printer. As with heat-transfer paper, the image or text must come from the computer. After printing, the freezer paper is removed. The results are usually very good; the fabric is softer than when using heat-transfer paper and the image is good quality, colourfast and can be washed normally. Commercially prepared cotton which has already been stiffened can also be purchased, giving similar results.

Opposite page and far right (detail):
High Life *(Sandra Meech). Night photos taken from the top of the Empire State Building in New York inspired the electric colours and the pattern, which echoes that of the streets below.*
Right: Two popular photo transfer methods: the acrylic mediums Picture This by Plaid and Image Maker by Dylon, plus Bubble Jet Set 2000.

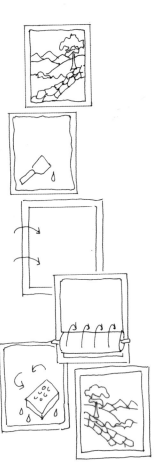

Acrylic medium is my preferred choice – I have been using it with success in my quilts for the last few years. You need a good laser-jet colour print in reverse or mirror image of the original from a professional copy shop. Both Picture This from Plaid and Image Maker from Dylon work in the same way. Pre-wash and dry white cotton fabric and then iron it onto freezer paper to keep the surface flat. Use a sponge applicator to spread the medium onto the colour copy about 2.5mm (⅛in) thick, so that you can no longer see the image. Quickly place the copy face down onto the prepared cotton, and gently press out any air bubbles. Leave for 48 hours in a warm,

dry place (it may appear crinkled and distorted), then remove the freezer paper and soak the whole piece in water for 15 minutes. Lay the fabric out flat on a smooth surface and use a household sponge to rub off the paper backing (about 90% is taken off the first time you do this). Drying will reveal an additional layer of fine paper, which will also need to be removed. Do not soak in water but gently remove the excess paper with the damp sponge. This method takes time but the results are very good. It does plasticize the cotton so it cannot be ironed and requires extra consideration during quilting, but the image will never fade.

Left: The step-by-step method for using acrylic medium.

Above: Results from various photo-transfer methods. Left to right: Heat transfer papers can result in an darker, duller image than the original; Acrylic medium gives true results but plasticizes the fabric; Bubble Jet Set 2000 gives good results but requires good quality home printing.

Above: A combination of commercial Bali and dyed fabrics can work successfully with diary writing and photo-transferred images.
Right: **Remembering Cabot** *(Sandra Meech).*
To an acrylic-painted background which shows the colours of the autumn landscape, I have added a mix of photo images of rock shards, lichen, and the harbour in St. Johns, Newfoundland, Canada.

PLASTICS

Plastics cannot be ironed and may have some limitations, but for contemporary quilts they offer many interesting effects. Options include laminating plastics to trap fabrics and mixed materials in wall hangings, or heavier plexiglass, which is often used for installations. For our purposes, however, materials found closer to home are easier to experiment with as they are readily available and can create interesting, layered surfaces for stitching by hand or machine.

Above: Fabric can be layered with plastics and other elements to create interesting effects.

Below: A selection of machine-sewn samples including both trapped and open surfaces with plastic.

Try using the following plastic materials:

• Bubble wrap, Clingfilm (Saran Wrap) and clear or opaque plastic bags.

• Metallic threads, stranded cottons, wools, fabrics, Lurex, net, lace or sequins.

• Sweet papers (candy wrappers), iridescent clear wrapping and metallic paper.

• Bonding or mending powder (finely cut Bondaweb (Wonder Under) will work).

• Baking parchment or a Teflon sheet to protect the iron.

• A painted, dyed or transfer-dyed surface as a starting point for colour.

• An iron (flat or dry steam) and ironing surface.

Try the following techniques:

▸ *Add cut pieces of threads, wools, paper sequins, metallic papers and so on onto the fabric, in a thin layer with a sprinkling of bonding powder. Cover with a double layer of plastic film or bubble wrap (bubbles face down) then top with baking parchment before ironing. This surface is sealed but care is needed when machine stitching. Use for wall hangings only.*

▸ *Lay out some bubble wrap, bubble side up, and cut up fine pieces of net, paper, threads, wool and fabric and so on, adding bonding powder on top. Cover with baking parchment and iron. This method results in a less stable surface, more suitable for hand stitching than machine stitching. A thin layer of chiffon can be added to make it more practical for sewing by machine and incorporating into art quilts.*

Opposite page: **Reflections on a Piece of Printed Fabric** *(Ann Fahy, Ireland). Mirrors, clear vinyl and printed cotton on linen squares.*

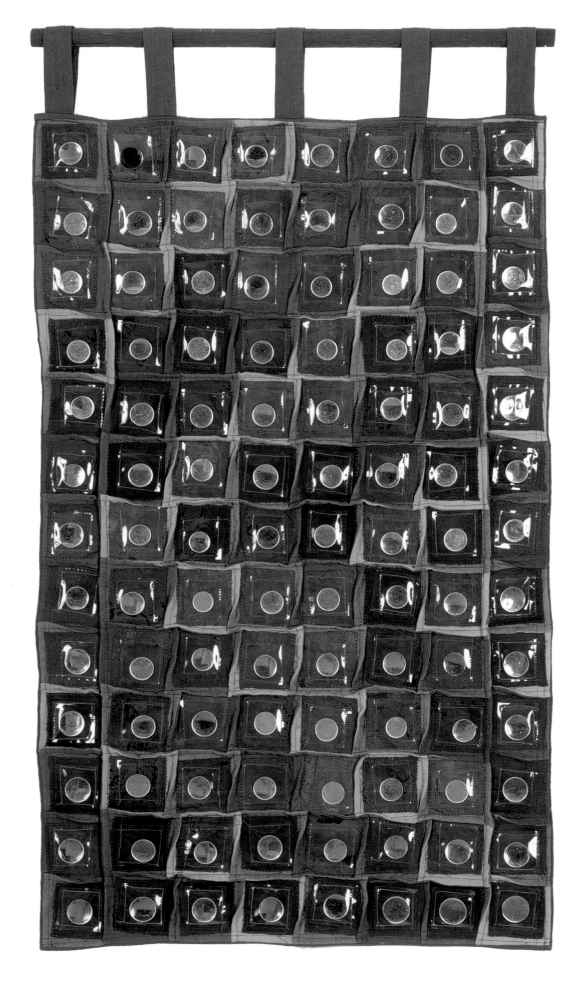

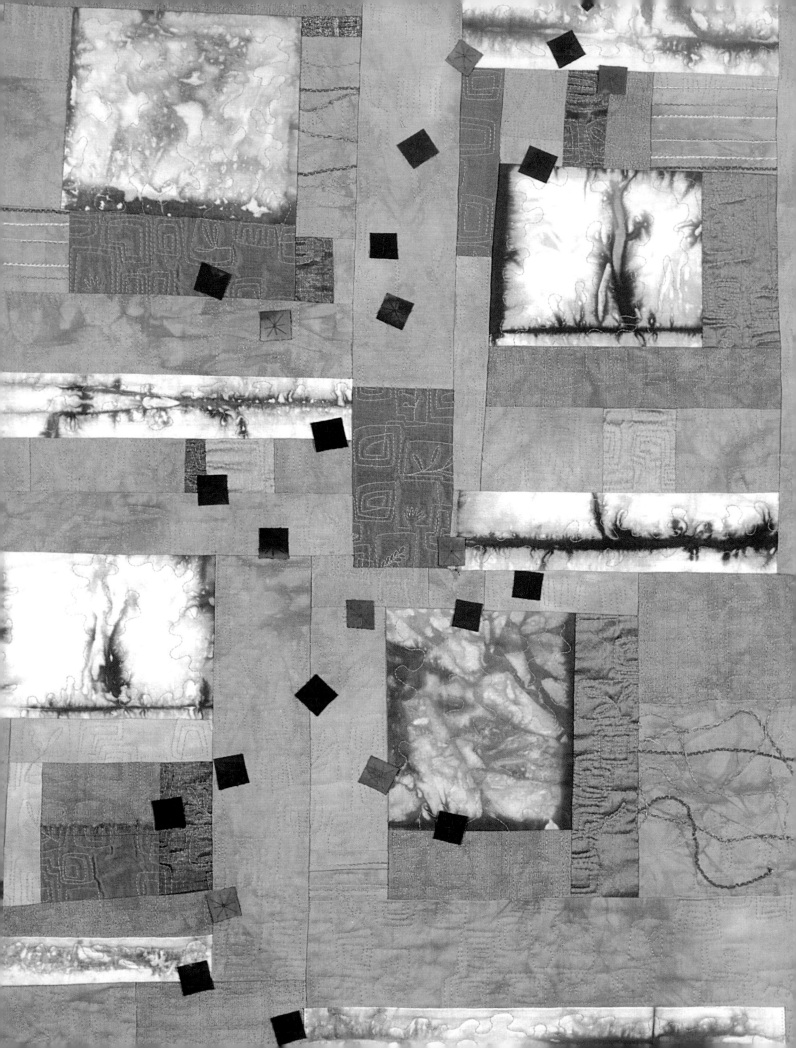

With a theme in mind, we have collected photographs and words of inspiration. We have made drawings, painted paper and fabric and created some collages – a wonderful array of materials for inspiration. What better place to display this information so that you can consider it at leisure than on a creative planning board or in a working design file? Both are a constant visual record to inspire and help with our design and colour decisions. If you have available space where you sew, a planning wall or bulletin board is a valuable way to collect information.

A working design file is smaller and is your own personal collection of ideas, papers and fabric swatches, which can be added to continuously. Use the window template from Design Class 1 to select an interesting area that could also become a starting point for a quilt design.

STAIRWAY SCREEN DETAIL, 78 DERNGATE, NORTHAMPTON

STAIRCASE, WILLOW TEA ROOMS, GLASGOW

Opposite page: **Iceland: The Lava Fields (detail)** *(Delia Salter, UK) Mosses and lichens of lava fields in September – the panels reflect hot springs and escaping steam, while the small squares remind the viewer of autumn's red berries.*

Above: A design board is an immediate visual record of design and colour information including fabric swatches and drawings for future reference. This board is based on the art, design and architecture of Charles Rennie Mackintosh.

Design Class 2 Creating a sketchbook

A sketchbook is the most portable way of keeping and recording information. It could contain a number of different themes and contain a mix of media approaches. Beginning with simple line drawings, through tone, texture and collage, you will have created a wonderful design journal with this step-by-step approach. A standard 15cm × 22cm (6 × 9in) landscape-format sketchbook is a practical size to carry.

Materials

The following list is a basic one, suitable for home or holiday use, but a smaller selection would be better to take to a museum or other place of interest.

• Sketchbook that includes a variety of sketching papers, white or cream cartridge paper, pastel Ingres and tracing papers. A spiral-bound book could include collage material and fabric samples.

• Set of watercolours or dyes (such as Koh-I-Noor) with a thick brush for wash backgrounds and a thin one for detail.

• Graphite pencils (HB to 4B), Conté pencils in black, brown and white, fine black pen, a putty eraser and craft knife.

• At least 12–24 blendable coloured pencils including white, plus some Aquarelle (water-soluble) pencils or sticks.

• A set of oil pastels for marks and resists.

• A viewfinder or window card to help focus on detail (see Design Class 1, page 24).

• Collage materials such as painted plain and textured papers, magazine papers, black-and-white and colour photocopies on your theme, in colours to complement.

• Glue stick, sewing kit and a small selection of threads.

• Matt varnish as a sealer (optional).

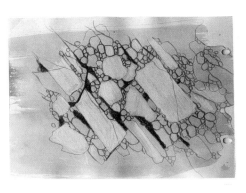

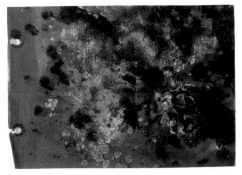

Method

1 The most daunting aspect of drawing is making that first mark on a white page. A possible first step is to paint on a wash in a pale or neutral colour, giving a starting point for what you are drawing (page 64, below left).

2 Use your favourite tools and follow the guidelines in Drawing and Mark-making (page 31). Fill the page completely and don't worry about your drawing extending into the gutter or onto the next page. Attach more paper to the side if you haven't enough room.

3 Torn, painted or textured papers, tissue or magazine sheets can re-create any image (page 64, middle left). Try a mosaic method with coloured magazine papers.

4 Stitch onto scrim (muslin) with stranded cottons, string or fine wools and add these (below), or use pieces of fabric.

5 Consider adding painted, black-and-white or coloured photocopies with written words (right). These can be torn or woven for interesting effects.

6 If desired, seal collage pages of mixed material with a matt varnish.

7 Although sketchbooks are personal, the overall impression can be important, especially if you are exhibiting your book. Cover it in collage, painted paper or fabric for a personal statement (page 64, top). Alternatively, you could bind your own pages using simple stab-bound methods, or investigate the craft of bookbinding for yourself. There is nothing more satisfying than creating your own book.

CHAPTER 3

DESIGN

In order to build confidence in creating new concepts for our quilt and textile designs we need to understand the design choices available to us. Concentrating first on the basic rules and principles of design, this chapter then looks at the main elements of design including colour, line, form, pattern and texture.

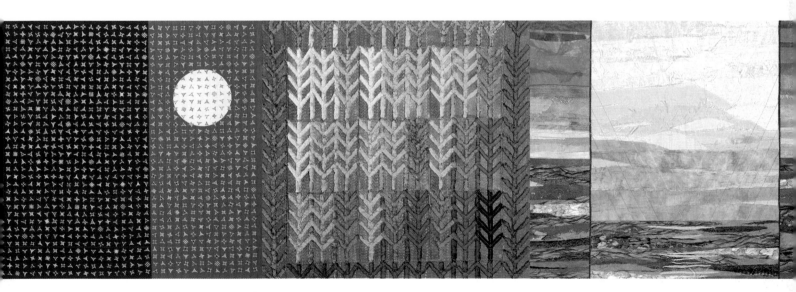

Opposite page: **Spring in Baker Lake (detail)** *(Sandra Meech). A composition of photo-transferred images: the hamlet and tundra near Baker Lake with the spring colours of moss and lichens showing through melted snow.*

Above and opposite page (detail): **Northern Reflections**
*(Sandra Meech). An early quilt inspired by life in Arctic
Canada. Although symmetrical in design, it has a
contemporary feel with the cut and pieced block rotated
on itself in the central motif and the applied images
around the edge. Appliqué with fusible web, satin stitch
embroidery and hand quilting.*

Design

There are some people who are lucky enough to come intuitively to design: they seem to know instinctively how to compose shape, where to add lines or marks and how to use colour without looking at the 'rules'. For the rest of us, however, it is important to realize that there are principles that can be learned and practised to inform our design and colour decisions. The overall visual effect of our work depends on a number of important factors including balance, focal point or centre of interest, and unity.

DESIGN PRINCIPLES

Balance

Unconsciously, we seek a visual balance in everything we look at, but it is often easier to see balance and harmony in nature and the world around us than create it in our contemporary quilt designs. Traditional quilts for beds were symmetrical, a perfectly balanced arrangement of blocks or a surface design around a central motif. The effect is ordered and pleasantly calm but often unadventurous. Our challenge is to gain the confidence to move into the abstract, producing a quilt design that may include irregular shapes and movement through line with varying proportions of colour. This is where balance becomes very important. Our artistic eye will need to equalize the composition, adding and subtracting shapes and lines to create visual harmony. Sometimes areas that are not equal create an unbalanced effect that can be strong and dynamic, creating a kind of tension across the design.

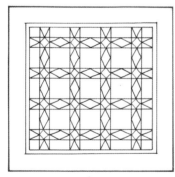

1.

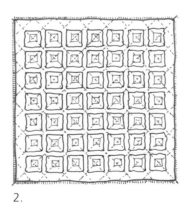

2.

3.

4.

5.

Above: Different quilt designs, including the traditional and symmetrical (1 and 2), a more transitional geometric design (3), a more painterly and abstract approach (4) and an unusual, shaped installation (5).

Unity

Another visual principle of design to consider is unity, when all aspects of the composition come together to make a cohesive design. When viewed, a quilt should sustain interest. Directional lines, rhythm, movement, and the use of colour and pattern all add together to make this happen. Every aspect of the design should belong and be related in some way to the next. This can be achieved with repetition (repeating shapes, colours, textures, pattern and line) or the placement of the individual elements in a related, cohesive arrangement.

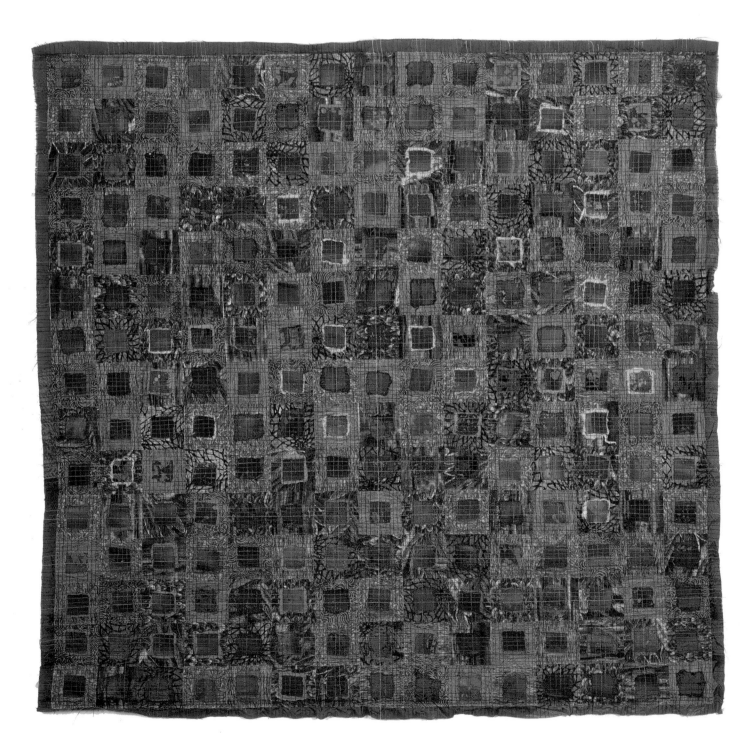

Focal point

The focal point or centre of interest is the area in our design that we want to emphasize, and where it is placed is an important factor in achieving good design. Colour, line, shape and pattern are important factors in this because they can draw the eye in as it moves across the surface of the quilt. An established design 'rule' to apply at this stage is the Rule of Thirds.

Opposite page: **Enmeshes IX** *(Sally-Ann Boyd, UK) Fabric and handmade papers machine stitched onto a rayon background.*
Below: **Sunform in Magenta** *(Fenella Davies, UK) This striking abstract design uses the rule of thirds.*

Artist's Hint The rule of thirds

When an area is broken into thirds, both horizontally and vertically, the area where two of the lines intersect is a place where focal points usually look right. Artists often place the horizon or top of a mountain range along one of the horizontal thirds, and they might place the edge of a building against one of the vertical thirds, for example. In a portrait, the face might be placed where two of the thirds intersect, and in abstract work you will often see a bright streak of colour or an important shape placed here. Apply this rule to photographs or magazine pictures and experiment with design principles in your own work.

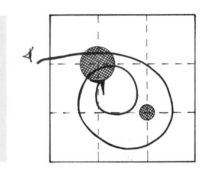

Once the focal area is chosen use colour, shape, directional lines or texture to bring the viewer from here into the overall surface design of the piece. Often one primary centre of interest is enough, but frequently a smaller, secondary focal point can help to balance the design. (It is worth noting that if there is a point of interest where all the lines intersect, the focus becomes central to the whole design and it becomes symmetrical.)

We learn to read from left to right in Western cultures, so a favoured place for a focal point is the top left-hand area – think about magazine and newspaper page layout and the position of the all-important photograph or headline.

Eastern cultures read from the bottom of a page, so their design orientation is quite different. Alternatively, an art quilt may not have a centre of focus at all, and instead have an overall pattern with an even distribution of colour, line or shape to create balance.

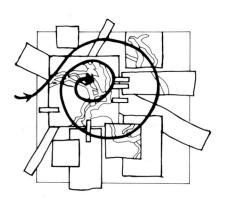

1.

2.

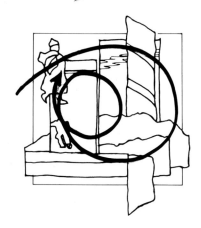

▶ Try cutting shapes and arranging them with the rule of thirds principles in mind. Start with a series of squares and rectangles and place them on an imaginary grid of horizontal and vertical lines with an important, colourful image as a focal point. Imagine what the same composition could look like translated into fabric. You could then try the same exercise, but using more random and irregular shapes. Here are two examples:

Composition 1: Vines

The strong diagonal crossed lines in this composition (above left) draw the eye immediately in. Square and rectangular

photographs of tree roots and vines are placed to curve around the surface, creating movement and interest. The red bars were added to create a sense of unity.

Composition 2: Bolivia

Photos of Bolivia create another interesting composition (above right), this time with irregularly shaped elements. The main focal point is the woman in the top left-hand corner, then the eye is brought into the textile design, down the pillar, and back to the man on the bench. The eye continues to find more interesting detail until the whole surface has been viewed.

Above: **One Circle, Three Colourways** *(Sara Impey, UK). This bold, asymmetrical design, overlaid with patterns of shape, colour and line, is a contemporary interpretation of the enduring and satisfying qualities of traditional quilts – elaborate surface with overall visual impact.*

ELEMENTS OF DESIGN

The elements of design covered in this section are categorized into line, shape and pattern. Line includes arrangements of lines into stripes, while under pattern I have included texture as a three-dimensional pattern.

Line

This is one of the most important elements of design and has been used in textile cultures through the ages. We begin the creative process using lines even at the planning or sketching stage; lines of all lengths and widths that give emphasis and meaning to our ideas. We can use them in an exaggerated form as a collage of strips that are parallel, curved, woven or repeated for more design possibilities. On fabric we can paint, piece or apply lines to the surface, then add further marks or quilting at a later stage.

Some lines are obvious visual elements of a design, and others are merely suggested or implied. They can become the outline of shapes, create zigzags or produce movement in spirals or waves. When sections of line are repeated, they become pattern. However lines appear, and in whatever form, they can communicate a vast number of emotions, feelings and attitudes as well as directing our eye into and around the surface of the quilt.

STRIPES

A surface can be divided into stripes of an equal width or a variety of widths, which can run horizontally, vertically or diagonally across a surface. They can be found everywhere in nature: on plants, insects, fish, mammals, rocks, and even our fingerprints as well as manmade impressions on the landscape such as ploughed furrows or skyscrapers.

Opposite page: **Arcticscape (detail)** *(Sandra Meech).* *Inspired by tundra in spring, this quilt uses strip piecing with trapped fabric and net fragments between plastic, stitched and machine quilted. Below: The inspiration for the quilt came from sketchbooks and photographs.*

Above: **Spiral Groove** *(Jane Lloyd, UK) In this striking design, the repeat spirals move forward and retreat, while the strips seem to dance. Layers of fabric are sewn together and cut to reveal colour and shape underneath.*

Right: The spiral is a strong image on its own. When the scale is reduced and a motif is repeated, a continuous overall pattern occurs.

USING PATTERN

There are some important things to remember when using pattern. These are scale, unity, balance and a sense of depth. Whether a surface fabric has been printed, painted, dyed or bought, the scale of the pattern will have a great impact on the design. The smaller the size, the less visible the pattern will be. The actual size of the piece of fabric also determines how visible the pattern is – large-scale patterns will not be seen if the piece is small. As well as bringing unity and balance to the design, pattern can also create a sense of depth. Patterns that are larger in scale will come forward and smaller, detailed patterns will recede. Finally, quilting by machine or hand can create another pattern that can be very different to the pieced surface design.

Above: **Church Wood** *(Dinah Travis, UK). The pattern of tree forms and the subtle use of colour gives strength and dimension to the whole textured surface in this quilt. The detail (left) shows layered and raw edge appliqué piecing and the dramatic use of mark-making big stitch quilting.*

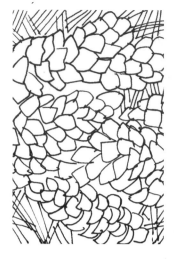

Texture

Pattern and texture often go together. With new materials and techniques in contemporary quilt-making, however, texture can be a separate design element, adding an extra dimension. Fundamentally, texture is the characteristic of the surface fabric: whether it is soft or smooth, rough or coarse. In the past, embellished quilts included raised embroidery, lace, velvets and silks, as well as trapunto-style quilting to add dimension to the surface. Today, contemporary quilters use additional techniques to create a textural quality. When planned into the design from the beginning, texture can make an unadventurous quilt exciting.

CREATING TEXTURE

There are many ways of creating texture that you could try. Here are some to get you thinking:

Quilting in all its variations. Quilting not only holds layers together but can also produce an independent design by adding a three-dimensional quality or creating movement across the surface.

Printed textured fabrics, either bought or created yourself. These offer a huge range of textures.

Photographic images transferred onto cotton. These can capture true textural realism for inclusion in contemporary quilts (see page 57).

Wools, stranded cottons and metallic threads with different weights and textures. These add interest and a tactile quality in addition to acting as a quilting stitch or decorative surface 'mark'.

Left: **Rock Face** *(Sandra Meech). A close-up photograph of a Spanish cliffside, revealing delicate plants in rock crevices, is surrounded by machine quilting that repeats the textures of the rock and plants, and photographic images.*

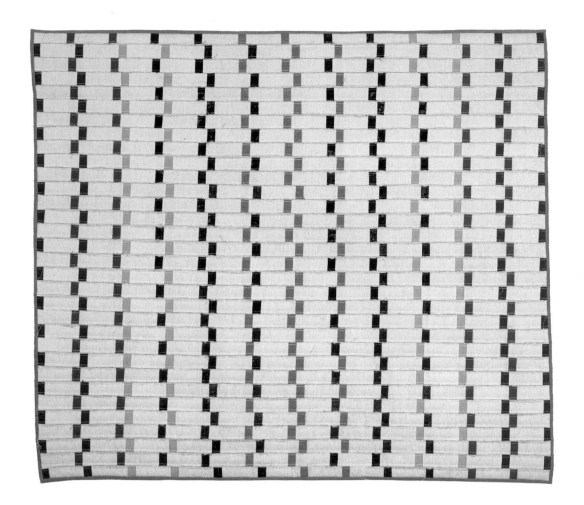

Left: **Els' Quilt** *(Inge Hueber, Germany) Strips and repeat colour reflect the Bauhaus principle 'less is more'. The strips are sewn together with raw edges on top, creating additional texture.*

Beads, buttons, ribbons, lace and fastenings add extra texture, enhancing the theme of the quilt.

Raw edge appliqué, layered sheers, scrims and lace also add to surface texture.

Three-dimensional appliqué, pleating and folding bring interest to your quilts.

Metals and plastics, which are also being used in contemporary quilt making (see page 60).

Right: **Spirits Soar (detail)** *(Sandra Meech). The middle section was quilted through wireform for dimension and includes copper and hand stitch.*

Above: **Tequila Sunrise**
(Christine Dobson, UK).
Sunrise reflected over the Gulf
of Mexico. Appliqué with raw
edges, cotton, lace, sheers
and free machine quilting
represent waves at sea.

Today we enjoy great freedom of expression in the quilting world, and what better time than now to take up the challenge of creating our own original designs. Contemporary quilts come in all sizes and you can practise a new theme, idea or design plan on a smaller scale. Practise some of the design exercises suggested and visit quilt shows to take a good look, make some notes and see which contemporary quilts use design and colour to best advantage.

Design Class 3 **Creative block design**

Here are two methods of working that will help you find a design suitable for a quilt. The first involves taking a pictorial reference, isolating an area, simplifying it and then moving it around and changing the colours to develop a block pattern for a quilt (see page 86 for illustrations of the various variations suggested here). The second method involves working directly from the source – a flower, collection of stones or whatever – and developing it either into a block pattern or a complete quilt design. Collections of shells, buttons, gourds, seedpods, ornaments or manmade objects, hubcaps, manhole covers or shoes could be your starting point.

Materials

- A photographic reference.

- Window templates (see page 24) with apertures of 2.5cm, 5cm and 7.5cm (1in, 2in and 3in) square.

- Tracing paper, layout paper or thin, opaque white paper.

- Magazine and painted papers.

- HB pencil, fine black pen, ruler.

- Coloured pencils (ideally a set of 24) and paint such as gouache, oil pastel or watercolour.

Rotated and repeated design

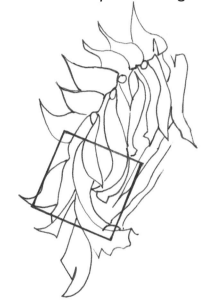

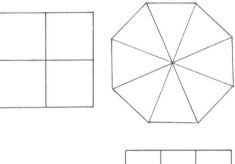

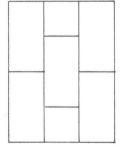

1 Choose a 2.5cm (1in) square of interest in your image (above). Trace it using a fine black line and simplifying the information (a on page 86). This first square is your master copy. Place a small arrow in the top left-hand corner (b).

2 Repeat the design twice in line (c), try a mirror image and then draw it again, this time filling in alternative areas in black. Create a counterchange effect by reversing the positions of black and white (d). Look for a centre of interest and consider if there are interesting lines, shapes or negative spaces.

3 Rotate the squares on themselves using the arrow as a reference as you rotate (e).

4 Change the corner that will be central to a new design. When blocks are rotated on themselves continuously, a natural symmetry to the whole design develops (f). Different apertures, perhaps triangular or pie-shaped wedges (template above and g) will multiply intriguingly, and it is worth trying a half-step rectangular block for variation (template above and h).

5 Now take your window template, angle it and lay it over any of the combinations you have made for a new slant (i).

6 Revisiting the first Design Class (page 24), you could extend these exercises further with colour and pattern (j).

CHAPTER 4
COLOUR

Design and colour go hand in hand in today's contemporary quilt world. If a quilt is poorly designed or does not use colour effectively, it will not catch the viewer's attention, regardless of how well it is made. This is just an introduction to the principles of colour but it will hopefully set you on the path of discovery, learning how new colour combinations can help stimulate an exciting design approach.

Opposite page: **Vertical Limit (detail)**. *(Sandra Meech). The diminishing icecaps meet urban living in this quilt on the theme of global warming. Photo-transferred images on a whole cloth cotton background.*

Colour

Understanding the principles and uses of colour and the basics of the colour wheel is the first step to using colour well. Once you start noticing and thinking about colours and colour combinations you will find that you start noticing it around you every day. Being observant like this is a constant challenge requiring continual practice, but you will find that you gain confidence all the way.

Opposite page: **This Season** *(Ann Fleeton, Ireland) The Mediterranean landscape in spring, with colours inspired by Pierre Bonnard's painting La Cote d'Azur. Hand-dyed linen and cotton with pleated silk.*
Above: A good selection of oil pastels is essential for colouring papers.

The meaning of colour

Our first impression of colour produces an immediate impact and reaction: it can make us feel calm, peaceful, disturbed or energized and invigorated. Our reaction to it is sparked off by several factors including resonances in nature (the colours in a butterfly's wing or a rainy day), past associations and our own cultural background. In ancient times it was considered to have mystical, divine and supernatural powers. Today, as we enjoy free colour choice and personal expression, it is important to understand the meaning of colour so we can determine how to use it effectively in our work. Here is a brief summary of the main colours:

Blue is the colour of the sky, mountains, lakes, seas, cornflowers and bluebells, each shade creating a different mood. Turquoise and aquamarine are both warm, happy, bubbly blues, while the cooler blues invoke a feeling of calm and peacefulness and greyed blues suggest sophistication. Blue decreases blood pressure and heart rate, encouraging a restful response, which is why it is such a favourite in bedrooms and bathrooms.

Green in found in lush gardens, rolling hills, plants, forests, moss or emeralds. It represents rebirth, regrowth, life, healing and rest as well as the freshness and joy of youth. It's an emotionally passive colour and is very relaxing.

Yellow evokes sunshine, daffodils, butterflies and harvest grains and has been an important colour in the history of many cultures. Gold is the most desirable metal and in China, yellow is an imperial colour. Yellow brings joy and happiness, lifting spirits as it heralds spring. However, yellow can also have negative meanings – treachery, envy and sickness.

Orange is seen in fruits, vegetables, flowers and in soils in the landscape, and gives a warm, earthy feeling. Autumn leaves, the pale colours of dawn and even the vibrant oranges of sunset give a feeling of security. Too much orange can be visually uncomfortable, but surrounding ourselves with orange can stimulate creativity and hunger.

Brown, which is often considered a neutral colour, is part of the orange colour family. Brown can stand for earth, chocolate and comfort, enhancing feelings of a natural, secure, trustworthy state, but it can also characterize melancholy and gloom.

Red appears frequently in nature: consider geraniums, poppies, roses, colourful birds, rubies and foods such as apples, tomatoes and cherries. Red is the most emotionally powerful colour in the spectrum, standing for sex, passion, excitement, anger, aggression, love, bravery and fire. Only a small amount will catch the attention, but being surrounded by red stimulates the brain, raises the blood pressure and quickens the pulse. A gentle version of red is soft, quiet, feminine pink, and other variations of red include magenta, crimson and reddish browns.

Purple as a pigment was difficult and highly expensive to obtain and so became a favourite of ancient rulers, representing wealth and nobility. There are many versions of purple, including violet, lavender and mauve, and in nature we think of spring flowers such as pansies, violets and irises. Feelings of love, courage, spirit and wisdom as well as sadness and mourning are often expressed with purple. The warmer versions of purple reflect royalty and grandeur and are used in ceremonial and religious attire.

Neutrals consist of white, black and grey. In the Western world, white stands for purity, cleanliness, chastity and cowardice. Black is symbolic of death, mourning and desolation but can also represent sophistication. Grey, neither positive nor negative, implies confusion, age, intelligence and work.

Colour moods

The 'temperature' of the colours selected for your design can create different feelings and emotional responses, setting a mood for the quilt. Warm colours, which are usually in the yellow to red area, can be light and bright, giving a sense of happiness and joy, or can be more intense, provoking anger or aggression. Cool colours, in the blue to green area, can be calm and serene when they are lighter, but sombre and sad in darker versions. Active colours are in the blue to red area with the stronger hues being more exciting. Passive colours are often found in the yellow to green zone: though if used in an intense way they can become active and vibrant. It is also worth exploring the relationships between colours and neutrals.

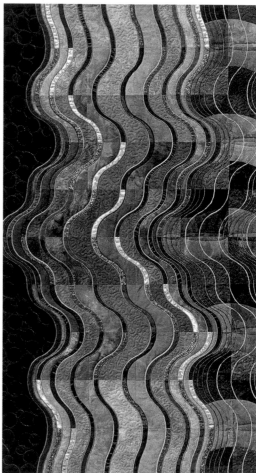

Above left: **Arctic Landscape 4** *(Bente Vold Klausen, Norway). Warm colours in a cold climate.*
Left: **Routes of Communication** *(Bridget Ingram-Bartholomaus, Germany). A dark, but vibrant use of colour accented by energetic movement.*
Above: **Waterfall** *(Susan Hagley, UK). Earthy colours are accented by the use of vibrant white silk.*

Left: **Woman and Vases** (Janet Twinn, UK).
Inspired by the figure, Greek vases and the
Mediterranean, the vibrant use of colour is a
dominating factor here. Top: **Atlantic City**
(Sandra Meech). The greys and beiges of winter,
highlighted with low sun on the boardwalk.
Above: **Journeys (detail)** (Sandra Meech).
Whites and ice blues give a cold feeling to photo-
transferred images.

Colour theory

Learning some colour terms will make it easier to understand colour descriptions and help identify the many qualities of colour.

Tints and tones of red

Hue is another word for colour.

Pure colour is the richest and clearest form of hue, with no other colours added – pure red, for example, rather than a bluish red or orange-red made by adding another colour to the basic red.

Primary colours are red, blue and yellow, and these are arranged in a ring on the colour wheel.

Secondary colours are green, orange and purple. These are made by mixing two adjacent primaries together – blue and yellow to make green, red and yellow to make orange, and red and blue to make purple.

Tertiary colours are the colours made by combining a secondary colour with the adjacent primary – blue-green, for example, or red-orange.

Value is the degree of lightness or darkness of a colour. A lighter value, called a **tint**, is made by adding white, while a darker value, called a **shade**, is made by adding black. A **tone** is the lightness or darkness of a colour. Imagine that you can see the colours in a black-and-white photograph or squint at them through half-closed eyes to help you identify the comparative tones of several colours.

Saturation is the degree of **intensity** of a colour that has had no white or black added – a colour at its most intense is said to be fully saturated.

COLOUR PALETTES

The range of colours chosen for a particular design is called the colour palette. Two of the most popular combinations are complementary colours and analogous colours, but there are others you might like to consider too.

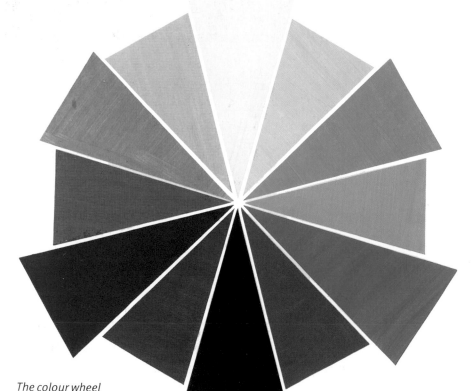

The colour wheel

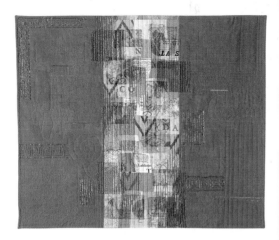

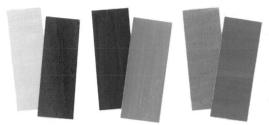

Complementary colours

Complementary colours are the colours that lie opposite each other on the colour wheel, such as red and green. In nature we see the red berries and green leaves of winter, the yellow and purple flowers of spring and the blues and oranges of tropical fish and sunsets.

Analogous colours are those that sit next to each other on the colour wheel, such as blue and green. This type of palette is a favourite when used with an accent of complementary colour – greens and blues with a touch of orange, for example,

yellow, orange and red with a sliver of cold blue, or red-purples and blues with a hint of lime green.

Chroma comes from the Greek word for colour and artists' colours with a high chroma are the brightest, most fully saturated ones. You might like to try a palette of bright colours for your quilt.

Achromatic means 'without colour'. Why not try a palette of white, grey and black? These neutrals are not colours, but they can make for a dramatic design or might provide a unifying background to the main colours of your quilt.

Monochromatic means using many values of one colour. This is daring but can work well.

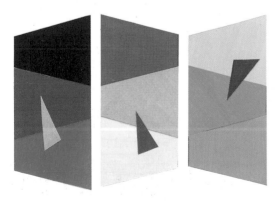

Analagous colours

Top left: **Roman Walls** *(Charlotte Yde, Denmark). Shades and tints of browns from the orange family create a collage of fabrics that include cut-back sheers. Writings and architectural detail are also used.*

Above: **Ice Floe (detail)** *(Sandra Meech). Complementary colours (blue and orange-brown) represent the Arctic landscape and caribou skins in this quilt.*

Colour relationships

In addition to setting the mood for your quilt design, colour can emphasize a certain area, drawing the eye to a centre of interest. Sometimes 'less is more': using a small amount of a contrasting colour can create a dramatic effect. Think of a scrap of pure yellow among a mass of blue fabrics, for instance, or a flash of red in a sea of green.

Warm and cool colours can be used together to create depth, the warm colours (including tints), coming forward while the cool colours recede. This not only means that red, orange and yellow seem to spring in front of blue and green, but, more subtly, a warm, reddish blue advances in front of a cooler, greenish blue.

Complementary contrast

Changes in the precise hue, intensity and value of a colour are influenced when colours appear next to each other. Our eyes play tricks with how we perceive colour and the colour contrasts that happen can be very dramatic and surprising. Understanding how this works can add to the overall strength of your design.

Contrasting values occur when light

colours are placed next to dark. A colour will look lighter against a dark background and darker against a light background. Another example of this is a white shape on a black background – it looks bigger than an identical shape in black, placed on a white background.

Contrasting colour with grey will also

show how a neutral colour is influenced by what it appears with. When a colour of medium intensity is placed next to areas of different colour strengths you will see a more intense colour contrast and this effect is often seen in contemporary quilts.

Contrasting colour with grey

Complementary contrasts occur when two colours opposite each other on the wheel are used together. In their pure form they are very bright but the 'greyed' colours – those that are made when the two are gradually mixed together – provide a new colour palette that can be used effectively and will enhance and support the two original choices. Artists describe these colours as having been 'knocked back' or muted.

Below: **Morning Star** *(Bobby Britnell, UK). Inspired by the rhythmic vitality of a Morris dance, this quilt explores pattern, colour and movement. The blue stars and spirals vary in intensity against a background of warm colours.*

Abstract design

1 Using the last exercise on the worksheet, start with the abstract window selection. Enlarge your design in line to fill a whole page. Make several copies.

2 Cut shapes from painted papers and magazine pages and apply them.

3 Try adding coloured tissue paper on the abstract shapes, looking at transparency.

4 Use fabric, either pieced or applied, to create a working sample. You may want to add net or sheer fabrics for interest. This could finally be quilted with mark-making stitches added as a starting point for a larger quilt.

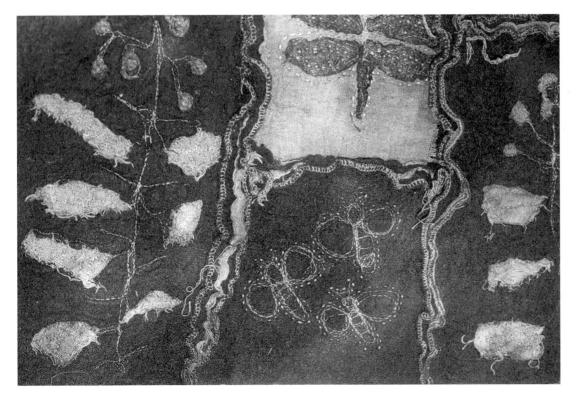

Above left: **Signs in Stone I**
(Bente Vold Klausen, Norway).
A strong, asymmetrical design
in blacks and whites.

Above: **Graffiti 8: Reindeer**
(Bente Vold Klausen, Norway).
Applied warm tundra colours
with a cold blue contrast acts
as a background for a strong,
linear reindeer design.

Left: **High Summer (detail)**
(Bailey Curtis, UK). Inspired by
summer garden colours, the
richness of the background
contrasts with the dyed and
frayed cotton, which has been
applied and stitched.

CHAPTER 5
STITCH

We all come to quilting from different backgrounds and with different aims in mind, and creating an art quilt that is original and personal is the most any of us can wish for. The confidence to take our inspiration through design and colour decisions to a final choice of materials is every quilter's challenge.

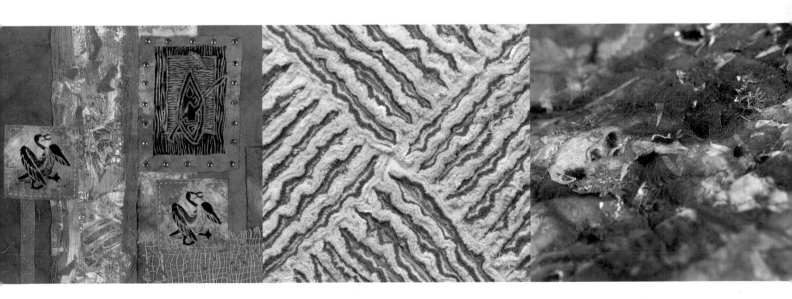

Opposite page: **Shoofly** *(Sandra Meech). This contemporary quilt is a celebration of the generations of Inuit seamstresses who have made caribou-skin clothing in such harsh climates. It includes the photo transfer of images and acrylic paintings with dyed and printed fabrics. Machine pieced and quilted. Collection of the American Craft Museum, New York.*

Stitch

These days we are not restricted to making practical quilts in 100% cotton fabrics. We can choose from a vast array of materials and employ various stitch techniques to create a quilt. Traditional methods of piecing, appliqué and quilting can be adapted to new surfaces including velvets, silks, sheers and plastics, with the addition of big stitch marks or metal. Our quilts can be shaped, dimensional and 'off the wall' or form a series of pieces on a theme. Our progress from early inspiration through design, colour and surface decisions will bring us to a stage where we need to choose methods of construction and, finally, the kind of stitch and embellishment to be used. This is perhaps the most rewarding stage of the process.

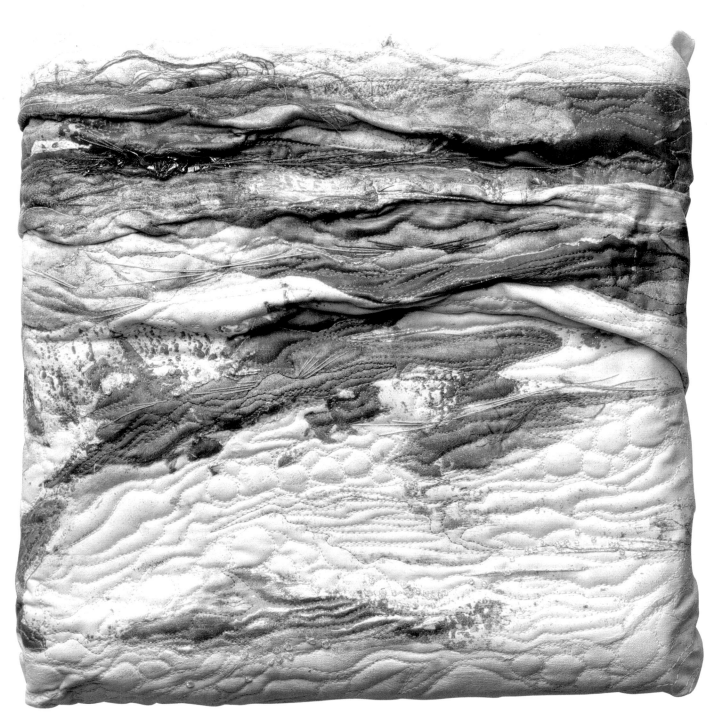

THE PLAN

Once we have our theme, have collected information and made our design and colour decisions, what comes next? First we must think about quilt size, shape and use, then select and decorate fabrics and other materials, decide on the method of assembly and, finally, add stitching and any other embellishments.

Quilt size and use

What will be the purpose of this quilt? What size and shape should it be? Is there a suggested theme? Will it be a small, experimental wall hanging, a larger art quilt for an exhibition or a more practical quilt that may need occasional machine washing? A small quilt that includes a mix of fibres, sheers, felt, paper or metal may be easily stitched by machine. With more control at this size, it could become a working sample for a larger piece or form part of a series. Larger exhibition quilts need different considerations. As dramatic wall hangings that dominate a space, they may be awkward and expensive to ship to exhibitions and be difficult to store. A practical first step could be to create a contemporary design for a lap quilt or bed throw. In this case fabrics need to be machine washable but they could include dyed and painted fabrics. A specific quilt theme could also dictate size and shape as well as fabric choices.

SHAPE

Would a shaped quilt be more dynamic? Irregularly shaped quilts can be very powerful in their space, but it is important to make early decisions about how they will be hung. Could there be sections cut out and how would these negative spaces be finished off – satin stitch or a raw edge? Being aware of these considerations will help you to analyse the quilts on display at the next exhibition you attend.

Opposite page: **Winter Sun** *(Sandra Meech). The last rays of the low, cold sun on the horizon. Transferred acrylic painting, quilted over wireform and shaped as a block. Machine quilted with metal and hand-stitching.*
Right: **Late Summer** *(Bailey Curtis, UK). A shaped textile made from pieced and applied felt.*
Far right: **Obi** *(Elizabeth Brimelow, UK). Hand-stitched and manipulated cloth, used for its tactile and intimate qualities.*

Left: Patterns stamped with discharge paste and pigment on black cotton velvet create some interesting surfaces (Frances Self).

Below: This felt machine-stitched sample uses an embroidery technique called faggoting, which could be used in contemporary quilting (Frances Self).

Fabrics

What materials will I use? The dyed, painted or bought fabrics to be used in the quilt must be created or collected at an early stage. Creating your own fabrics is satisfying and can give strong impact to the design. These fabrics can be skilfully pieced alongside commercial fabrics purchased from shops or over the Internet. Consider Bali, batik or natural-texture prints or look for world textiles – try Japanese, African or Australian – to add to your collection. Experimenting with photographic transfer or using plastics and layering with sheer fabrics may take extra planning but these will add extra dimension and interest. It may also be a good idea to consider heavier fabrics like wool and felt, which are often seen in contemporary quilting today. Bleaching and discharge methods on cotton and velvet for shape and pattern also require extra time to explore. Preparing these fabrics and achieving the desired results is part of the challenge we all face.

Opposite page: The range of fabrics available today is diverse: metallic polyester voiles, shiny printed jerseys, African batiks or Bali fabrics can all be mixed with our own dyed, painted, printed or commercial cottons.

Felt and fleece are readily available. Fleece has always been popular for children's cuddle quilts and wearable garments, and as a fabric it is easy to piece and sew. Quilt stores often stock some of these along with commercially dyed felt in different weights that give real dimension when used in appliqué. Many folk patterns adapt well to these types of fabrics, including applied shapes in wool with embroidery stitches in stranded cotton.

Creating your own felted fabrics from wools and silk tops is an option that can be fun. These can be stitched in a pattern or layered with sheers with sections cut back through. Most felts can be machine pieced and stitched depending on the thickness, and hand-quilted marks can be especially effective on felt. Quilts made from felted blankets and knitwear (in natural fibres) have also become popular. However, these new felted fabrics can become very dense and the quilts will be heavy.

Above: Colourful contemporary felt samples. Inspired by folk patterns, hand-felted and commercial blanket fabrics are applied with decorative embroidery stitch. Dyed cotton felt with applied and cut-back sheers create the medieval floor tile piece (Jenni Last).

Chenille is an exciting option. The layering and stitching of cotton with unusual fabrics in different colours makes a wonderful texture when the layers have been cut back and frayed. Each sample is unique, making chenille a technique that has become very popular again.

Glimmering fabrics add another dimension. Consider using shot or two-way silk or Lurex that catches the light in different ways, or metallic fabrics to add shine and glitter.

Dyed fabrics can be as dynamic as you like, and you don't have to limit yourself to plain cotton. Cotton or silk velvet will take dyes, fabric paints and sticks, and images or patterns from a block or stencil can be bleached or discharged for interesting effects. Polyester velvets, voile and lace can be transfer dyed, but extra care is needed when ironing polyester fibres as many snag and fray easily, so experiment with these fabrics first. Remember, sometimes less is more.

Heavy interfacings are being used in quilting to emphasize shaped pieces or to add structure to quilts used as installations. They can be painted or transfer dyed, but on a large scale they are awkward to stitch with a conventional sewing machine. Interfacings like pelmet or craft Vilene prevent a quilt from being rolled so it would need to be kept flat for transport to exhibitions. For *The Five Days in May: Pages from an Arctic Journal* (page 112), I used heavy Vilene for the diary writing (with transfer-dyed colour), wadding in the middle and a transferred photograph or fabric layer on top. All the segments were satin stitched and hinged with string in a herringbone stitch to fold as 'pages'.

Wadding for quilts comes in different thicknesses and contains either polyester or natural fibres – it is a matter of personal choice. The thinner 100% cotton varieties dye well and create raw-edge effects if desired. Cotton wadding is easy to stitch through for both machine and hand quilting, and it may be worth revisiting traditional techniques with trapunto wools that are added to the middle layer for extra dimension in a modern quilt. For the plasticized photo-transferred images used in quilts, a thicker wadding may be necessary to emphasize the machine-quilt lines.

Soluble fabrics are hot and cold water-soluble materials that come in either clear film, fabric or paper varieties. With free-motion embroidery techniques they can create open, lacy thread layers or denser, more solid shapes. These can be pieced or applied onto a quilt surface, giving extra dimension.

Above: This chenille sample shows the wonderful pattern and textural qualities that can be achieved with this technique (Gill Knight).

Above: **The Five Days in May: Pages from an Arctic Journal** *(Sandra Meech). Rock, Ice, Skin, Hamlet, Tundra. Inspired by diary writing and photographs taken in the Inuit communities of Baker Lake and Rankin Inlet in northern Canada, this quilt shows how effective working in a series can be.*

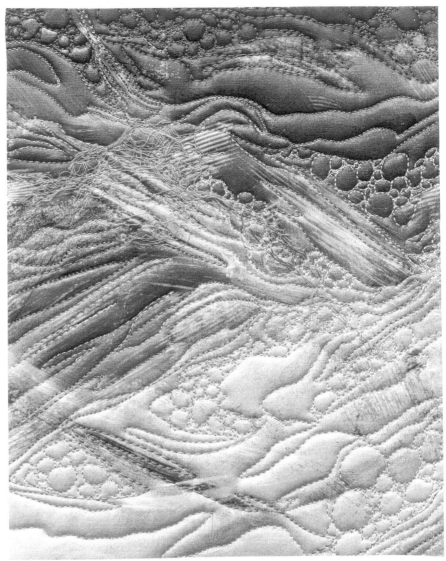

Plastics, including Clingfilm (Saran Wrap), bubble wrap and clear bags, can be used to trap and bond fabrics and threads together (see page 60). This material reflects light and can be an interesting addition to conventional piecing. Plastics will dull machine needles quickly, cannot be ironed and are usually limited to wall hangings only but they can work well. In 'Arcticscape' (page 74) a strip layer of bonded plastic has been used to represent ice on the tundra.

Handmade or fibre papers are also
finding their way into contemporary quilt mixed-media hangings. These textile pieces may have two or three layers like a quilt but are more of a 'fibre art' textile in nature. Nevertheless, the boundaries are shifting in the world of contemporary quilt-making and new materials are to be celebrated.

Acrylic paint is finding its way into the quilt
scene (see page 37). Broad brushstrokes and washes can be dramatic, but with thicker paint care is needed when piecing and stitching. Acrylic paint or the medium used in photographically transferred images will all stiffen cotton and blunt machine needles quickly.

Silk-screen printing to create colour and pattern on cloth provides another approach worth consideration. Modern artists who exhibit widely in galleries everywhere have been using screen printing on cloth incorporating minimal stitch with mixed media. We can do the same, with more layers and dimension, in our contemporary quilts.

Above left: Stitching through a combination of dyed, painted and metallic fabrics with handmade and magazine papers can extend ideas and is always worth a try.

Above: **Towards the Sun (detail)** *(Sandra Meech). Acrylic paint on cotton reflects the golden colours in the Arctic spring.*

QUILT ASSEMBLY

Which techniques should you use for assembling your quilt – strip piecing, a created block, an abstract design in layers or a reverse appliqué? Often a theme will dictate the choice. Think about the piecing methods you are comfortable with, take them further with your own design and fabrics or try something new.

Opposite page: **Summer Camp** *(Sandra Meech). Lino-cut images on dyed cotton, machine collage with paper and sheers, and raw edge scrim and muslins are finished off with rough hessian and paperclips. Below: Detail of* **Els' Quilt.** *(page 83).*

There are many articles in quilting magazines and books showing piecing, appliqué and quilting techniques. This chapter reviews the basic assembly methods, putting greater emphasis on more creative approaches. Whatever way you decide to piece your quilt, workmanship is always important. Seams must be stitched accurately, with points, lines or design elements matching to the best of your ability. The more interpretive styles of quilt-making still have to conform to the essence and integrity of your theme. Whether a quilt requires simple or more complex piecing, a practice sample is always necessary. This can prove to be valuable, with problems revealed and solved straight away. Although contemporary in appearance, many modern quilts are made with very traditional piecing methods.

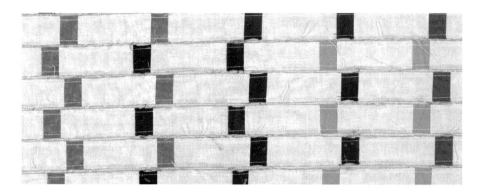

Piecing

Straight line and strip piecing using the

quarter-inch seam allowance was probably the first piecing lesson you learned, and it is still the most popular. Traditionally, the quarter-inch seam allowance was used to sew squares, rectangles and strips of fabric together in straight lines. Originally hand piecing, though time-consuming, was the most practical method, but today, machine piecing has taken over in popularity. With 6mm (¼in) machine feet to help with piecing, accurate seams are not too difficult to achieve.

▸ *Try strip piecing using several types of surfaces such as plastics, painted and dyed fabrics and coloured paper. Cut them into strips of different widths and combine. (See* Arcticscape, *page 74, which incorporates bonded plastic).*

Curved piecing over paper is another

popular option. Two adjacent curved sections of fabric are sewn together using a paper template method. A freezer-paper template can be ironed either onto the back or on top of the fabric before turning under. (If it is ironed onto the back, the design is reversed.) Remember, the fabric is 6mm (¼in) larger for the seam allowance. Using register marks for accuracy, wide curves can be easily managed by machine, but tighter ones may need hand piecing.

▸ *Try creating one of the design blocks made in Chapter 3 as a 30cm (12in) block using paper-piecing methods.*

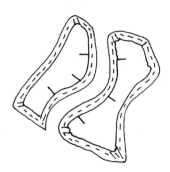

Above: Strip piecing with 6mm (¼in) seam allowance; Curved piecing over papers, for either machine or hand piecing.

Appliqué

Appliqué in many forms was one of the first methods of decorating a fabric surface. From early *Broderie perse* in the 16th century to modern layers in contemporary quilts today, the applying of fabric stitched in place has always been popular. There are many styles of appliqué that are seen in contemporary quilting that are based on traditional techniques but have an exciting modern twist.

Broderie perse is a traditional option. Details of flowers, birds, landscape or decoration on early printed cottons were applied in sections to a neutral background to produce a quilt design. For a more contemporary variation, sections of transferred photographs or paper images could be cut out and sewn into a design.

Appliqué over paper, familiar in Baltimore quilt styles with fruit, vines, flowers and historic symbols, has paved the way for more creatively designed images which find their way into quilt making today. Firstly, shapes are cut as paper templates (freezer paper is used today), then the fabric is cut 6mm (¼in) larger all round, turned under, and tacked (basted). Each section is individually applied to a background with a small, invisible blind stitch. Today in modern quilts any design element can be applied in the same way. In *Northern Reflections* (page 68), Bondaweb (Wonder Under) was used to iron images in place before they were satin stitched together.

Reverse appliqué is another method that has been used for centuries in many parts of the world which employs several layers of different fabrics (Mola work from Central America is one example). Two popular ways of using reverse appliqué are given here. Try either of these methods with some wonderful surfaces created with fabric paints for interesting results.

▶ *Machine stitch the design from the back (design in reverse) through all the layers. From the front, cut away different sections or colours using fine scissors and trimming right up to the stitch line. Machine satin stitch can be worked from the top over the raw edges to hide the seam and bring the design together.*

▶ *Draw your design on the surface of the top layer. Tack (baste) all the layers together. Cut away different sections leaving at least 3mm (⅛in) extra for turning under with a small, invisible stitch.*

Appliqué in layers is one of the more popular methods in contemporary quilting. The addition of sheers, muslins, net or lace to a fabric surface can create texture or transparent effects and mixed media, metal, paper or trapped plastics could be added for interest. Raw-edge appliqué can give texture and dimension and has been accepted now as another method in contemporary quilt-making.

▶ *When visiting the next contemporary quilt exhibition, make a record of all the different styles of appliqué you can find.*

Left: These details of **Church Wood** *(Dinah Travis) (page 81) and* **Northern Reflections** *(Sandra Meech) (page 68) show two very different methods of appliqué.*

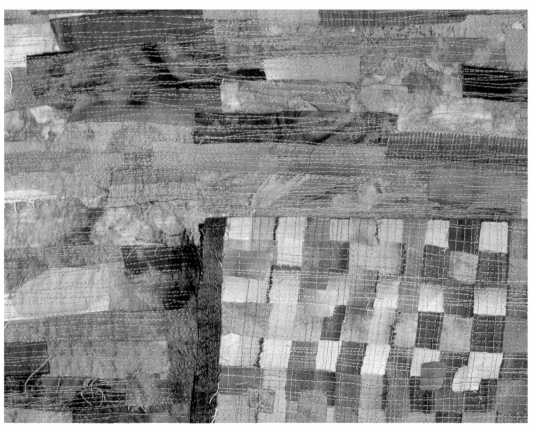

Above left: **Elseverywhere**
*(Dirkje Van der Horst-Beetsma,
Netherlands). Images of metal,
ripped to reveal the soft, warm
contrast beneath. The red
batik and screen-printed fabric
was created by Els Van Baarle.*
Left: **Interwoven (detail)**,
*(Dirkje Van der Horst-Beetsma,
Netherlands). Layers of
mixed, dyed fibres are
collaged together and
machine quilted. The use of
hot colours gives contrast.*
Above right: detail of **Obi**
*(Elizabeth Brimelow, UK). The
stitches resemble man's
'marks' on the landscape.*

STITCH TECHNIQUES

Gone are the days when quilters were criticized for using the sewing machine for quilting. Free-motion machine quilting is now firmly established as a way to stitch through layers. In contemporary quilt art, big-stitch hand quilting is also seen as a new way of making expressive marks on the surface. The most exciting trend recently is for a mixture of both free-machine 'interpretive quilting' and hand stitch, and for embellishment with metal or beads.

Styles of machine quilting

Machine quilting has always been popular for straight-line, in-the-ditch styles of quilting on a traditional heirloom quilt pattern and the later stages of sewing on a quilt binding. Today, however, there are many more quilting styles to choose from. Machine quilting can be used to contour applied shapes or images, or act as individually drawn marks or a pattern of lines that is very different from the surface design. It could also be used in an interpretive, free-motion style that gives movement and dimension across the surface. Remember, acrylic on cotton, plastics and some photographically transferred cloth is thick and will blunt machine needles quickly. Machine quilting produces a clean and accurate line at the expense of a harder, firmer-looking surface in the finished quilt.

▸ *Make your first experiments with machine quilting on random-dyed or transfer-dyed surfaces and Bali or batik-style prints.*
▸ *Use small, experimental quilts in new surfaces to take your experiments further.*

Free motion machine quilting is more popular than ever. Your sewing machine should have a drop feed facility to cover the teeth, a variable top thread and bobbin tension, and a darning, embroidery or quilting foot (one with an open end will allow for greater visibility).

Machine embroidery threads or polycotton threads are best to start with: numbers 30 and 40 are good for machine quilting. Use needle sizes 70–110 or special machine embroidery needles.

For practice, try layering a fabric sample:
▸ *Sit comfortably, with the sewing machine slightly tilted forward to increase your viewing area. Thread the machine.*
▸ *Set the machine on straight stitch, with the stitch length and width at zero.*
▸ *Loosen the top tension slightly and set the 'needle down' position, if you have one on your machine.*
▸ *With the darning or quilting foot in place, begin working on your sample. Start the machine and keep to an even speed while moving the fabric gently around the surface. Practise for several minutes and correct the tension if necessary.*

Hand quilting

Our first efforts at quilting are usually by hand but with today's busy lifestyles many of us don't enjoy this satisfying experience by making the time for hand quilting. This is a shame because we miss out on the immediate response to the feel of the needle as it moves through layers of cloth. Recently, quilting as a decorative design element has brought us back to working with hand stitch or 'mark-making', alongside machine quilting, with the addition of extra embellishment.

Big-stitch quilting is now an option. It is not longer always necessary to make such small and delicate stitches, and big-stitch marks can be made next to seeding stitches that merge design or colour elements together, using a greater selection of threads, perhaps variegated, twisted or metallic.

Embroidery stitches of various types can be used together for a modern look. Tying a quilt or using French knots could be combined with other simple embroidery stitches such as herringbone or blanket stitch to add interest (see illustration, bottom right for some examples). Alternatively, try couching thicker wools or twisted fabrics onto the surface for added dimension.

Above: **Remembering Cabot (detail)** *(Sandra Meech). The photo images of houses and rock shards are continued in the quilting stitch.*
Below left: Big-stitch marks, couching, French knots and blanket stitch.

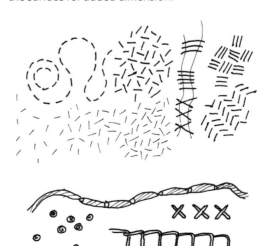

Embellishment

When stitching is completed and a binding has been finished, it is a good plan to 'live' with your wall hanging for a while to see if extra embellishment should be added. Sometimes stitch is enough, but there are ways we can add interest to an otherwise flat surface.

▸ *Sprinkle on some beads to add lustre and detail to a flat quilt surface. Letting them fall at random will give a good placement. Stitch them on with a beading needle or fine quilting between needle.*

▸ *Add bits of metal to the surface because this can strengthen a theme as well as catch the light. Most thin metals can be stitched by machine.*

▸ *Piece quilt sections together with fastenings such as safety pins, paper clips or metal wire.*

▸ *Add iridescent, pearlized or metallic acrylic fabric paints after machine quilting for extra texture, dimension and lustre.*

Opposite page: A surface created with bonding over plastic and wool.

*Above: Detail of **Containment** (page 51) showing iridescent plastic between threads.*

Artist's Hint Stitch samples

Many of the samples created as we progress through this book, from surface painting and design to quilting and the notes accompanying them, will become important reference for future projects. These can be documented in a sketchbook or a ringbinder for the future. Some of the larger samples could be used for a practical project such as a book cover (see picture below), pincushion, needle or glasses case, a framed stitch painting or gift card.

Design Class 5 **Inspired landscape**

A favourite inspirational theme is the landscape. This Design Class can begin with a photograph taken at home or on holiday, or selected from a magazine. The finished project will be a long and thin mixed-media piece that could stand on its own as a small piece of quilt art or be a starting point for a larger contemporary quilt.

Materials

- A landscape photograph that has distant views and interest in the foreground.

- Thin white card in L-shapes to make a window aperture large enough to accommodate your photograph.

- White copy paper and tracing paper.

- Black pens and pencils.

- Cutting board, craft knife, scissors and glue stick.

- Any of the surfaces listed in chapter 2 – painted, textured papers, dyed and painted fabrics, commercial fabrics, bonded and trapped in plastic surfaces, acrylic on Bondaweb (Wonder Under) – in colours sympathetic to your photograph.

- Thin piece of wadding, cotton, fleece or felt as a firm background.

- Sewing machine with machine threads.

- Hand-sewing kit (fine scissors, pins, needles).

- Wools, scrims, lace, beads.

Method

1 Use the L-shaped frames vertically to find an area in the photograph where the land is broken into a variety of shapes with movement and interest in the foreground.

2 Mark this area for reference and trace through the basic line shapes, keeping the detail simple.

3 Using an A4 (8½ x 11 in) sheet of paper, scale the small traced image up to fill the page with a black pen line.

4 Fill in the spaces with pattern, parallel, diagonal, wavy and crosshatched lines or circles, triangle or square shapes for texture.

Left: A selection of surfaces inspired by colours and textures in the landscape, including acrylic paint on fusible web, transfer dyes on net and interfacing, and painted textured papers and newspaper.

5 Go to your paper and created fabric surfaces, and cut, overlap and pin them in position on the background wadding or felt. Don't forget to use transfer-dyed fabrics, some with words, as well as the transfer-dyed papers.

6 Use an open zigzag stitch to keep the pieces in place before sewing a tighter satin stitch.

7 Use hand stitch for additional marks in the landscape, add beads or couch on textural materials in the foreground.

8 Think about whether you want to keep the edges irregular or frame the piece as a stitch painting. This could also be a working sample for a larger contemporary quilt.

Right: The landscape is finished with satin stitch and free-machine quilting. As a small working sample for a larger contemporary quilt, it could also be framed as stitched art.

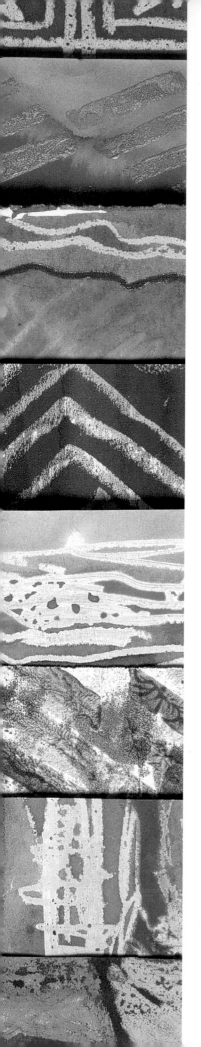

In conclusion

Traditional or contemporary, whatever background or level of quilting experience we have, from time to time we all need help in making decisions. There is a sequence of stages we can review if we want to continue to create original quilts. From that inspired spark of an idea through to design, colour and stitch choices, we make a journey that should be satisfying and rewarding as well as fun. By being aware of all the possibilities, opening ourselves to experimentation and new challenges, we will definitely move forward in our work. By regularly referring to this book and enjoying the workshops, I hope you will find greater confidence in your own contemporary quilt-making.

IMPORTANT STAGES TO REMEMBER

Ideas

How can sources of inspiration be found?

▶ *Decide whether you want to create a single project or a series of work.*

▶ *A theme or subject can come from many sources – some make themselves obvious to you, and others need to be 'discovered'.*

▶ *Sketchbooks: create drawings, paintings, writings, and collages to explore colour, texture and pattern through detailed observation.*

▶ *Photography: Your own pictures capture the moment, or the detail needed for reference – a great way to collect visual information.*

▶ *Words and thoughts: Diary-writing or poems can be emotional responses to an important issue, adding strength to your textile work.*

▶ *Books, magazines, newspapers and the Internet can be rich sources of material.*

▶ *Exploring surfaces in paper and cloth can also influence the final presentation.*

Design and colour

What are the best approaches to designing a contemporary quilt?

▶ *Consider the rules of composition and the elements of design to give pattern, texture, unity and colour in your working design plan.*

▶ *It helps to determine early the purpose of the piece and its size and shape.*

▶ *Choose the style of the contemporary quilt you want to make, perhaps using a creative block or an overall abstract design.*

▶ *Review colour theory to gain confidence in fabric or surface decisions.*

Surfaces

How can the fabric and surfaces for the project be collected or created?

▶ *Originate your own surfaces by dyeing or painting fabrics.*

▶ *Create mixed media surfaces with photographic transfer methods, bonding with plastics or quilting through wire.*

▶ *Search for creative commercial fabrics – Bali, batik or ethnic fabrics can look wonderful.*

Piecing and stitching

What piecing and stitching methods will be used?

▶ *Try traditional piecing or appliqué methods with a contemporary flair.*

▶ *Use new surface fabrics and raw edge approaches, combining mixed media.*

▶ *Decide whether you want to use hand or machine quilting and embellishment.*

Design Class 1 worksheet

This worksheet is to be used for the 'Looking Through a Window' Design Class on page 24. It can be photocopied.

PLACE YOUR

PHOTO SOURCE

HERE

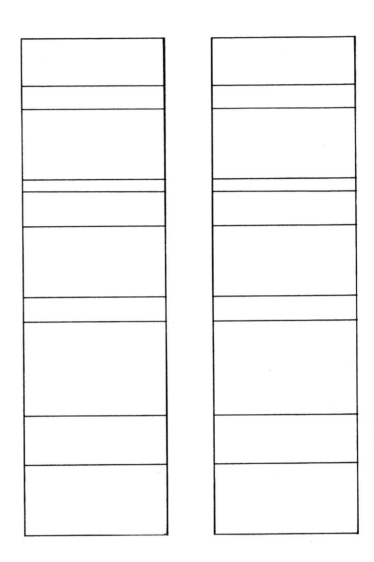

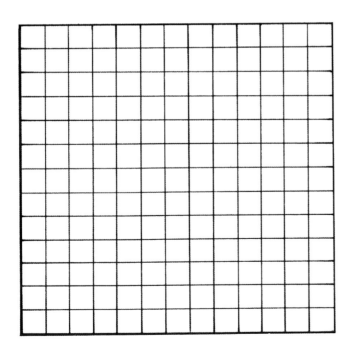

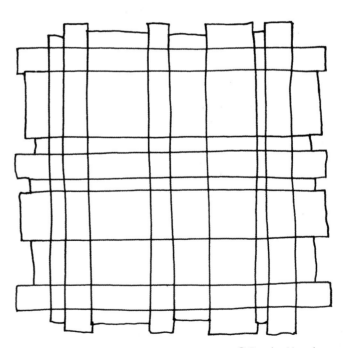

© Sandra Meech 2003

Design Class 3 worksheet

This worksheet is to be used for the 'Creative Block Design' Design Class on page 85. Again, it can be photocopied.

Recommended Reading/Supplier List

Recommended Reading

PHOTO TRANSFER

Laury, Jean Ray. *Imagery on fabric*. C&T
   Publishing, 1997.

Laury, Jean Ray. *The photo transfer
   handbook*. C&T Publishing, 1999.

SURFACES

Curtis, Bailey. *Dyeing to colour*. Bailey
   Curtis, publisher, 2001.

Dunnewold, Jane. *Complex cloth*. Fibre
   Studio Press, 1996.

Green, Jean Drysdale. *Arteffects*. Watson-
   Guptill Publications, 1993.

Issett, Ruth. *Colour on paper and fabric*.
   B T Batsford, 2000.

Issett, Ruth. *Glorious papers*. B T Batsford,
   2001.

Johnston, Ann. *Colour by design*. Ann
   Johnston, publisher, 2001.

Kemshall, Linda. *Color moves*. That
   Patchwork Place, 2001.

DESIGN

Brommer, Gerald. *Collage techniques*.
   Watson-Guptill Publications, 1994.

Jerstorp, Karin and Eva Kohlmark. *The
   textile design book*. A & C Black, 2000.

Johnston, Ann. *The quilters' book of
   design*. Quilt Digest Press, 1999.

Oei, Loan and Cecile De Kegel. *The elements
   of design*. Thames and Hudson, 2002.

COLOUR

Feisner, Edith Anderson. *Colour*.
   Laurence King, 2001.

Wolfrom, Joen. *Color play*. C&T
   Publishing, 2000.

STITCH

There are numerous books on the market
on patchwork, quilting, applique and
embroidery techniques. I particularly
recommend:

Beaney, Jan and Jean Littlejohn. *A
   complete guide to creative embroidery*.
   B T Batsford, 1997.

Beaney, Jan and Jean Littlejohn. *Stitch
   magic*. B T Batsford, 1998.

Burbidge, Pauline. *Quilt studio*. The Quilt
   Digest Press, 2000.

Hedley, Gwen. *Surfaces for stitch*.
   B T Batsford, 2000.

CONTEMPORARY QUILTS

Laporte, Gul. *Quilts from Europe*. C&T
   Publishing, 2000.

Fibrearts Design Book series, Lark Books.

Also recommended:

The Textile Directory
107 High Street, Evesham WR11 4EB
Tel: 0870 220 2820
www.thetextiledirectory.com

Supplier list

Art Van Go (colouring papers and cloth)
The Studios, 1 Stevenage Road,
Knebworth, Hertfordshire SG3 6AN.
Tel: 01438 814 946
www.artvango.co.uk

Rainbow Silks (silk fabrics and paints)
6 Wheelers Yard, High Street, Great
Missenden, Buckinghamshire HP16 0AL
Tel: 01494 862 111
www.rainbowsilks.co.uk

Colourcraft (Brusho powder paint)
Unit 5, 555 Carlisle Street East,
Sheffield S4 8DT
Tel/Fax: 0114 242 1431
www.colourcraftltd.com

Kemtex Colours (transfer dyes)
Chorley Business and Technology Centre,
Euxton Lane, Chorley, Lancashire PR7 6TE
Tel: 01257 230 220 fax: 01257 230 225
www.kemtex.co.uk

Omega Dyes (fabric and transfer dyes)
Myrtle Cottage, Powerstock,
Bridport, Dorset DT6 3TD
Tel: 01308 485 242
www.omegadyes.co.uk

Freudenberg Nonwovens (interfacings)
Lowfields Business Park, Elland,
West Yorkshire HX5 5DX
Tel: 01422 327 900
www.nonwovens-group.com

Whaleys (Bradford) Ltd (fabrics)
Harris Court, Great Horton,
Bradford BD7 4EQ
Tel: 01274 521 309
www.whaleys.co.uk

The African Fabric Shop (Fabrics)
Magie Relph, 19 Hebble Mount, Meltham,
Holmfirth, West Yorkshire HD9 4HG
Tel: 01484 850 188
www.africanfabric.co.uk

Index